In Search of Hamilton Burger:
The Trials and Tribulations of a Southern Lawyer

By Bill Haltom

BAPress

In Search of Hamilton Burger:
The Trials and Tribulations of a Southern Lawyer

By Bill Haltom

In Search of Hamilton Burger:
The Trials and Tribulations of a Southern Lawyer

TBAPress
Published by the Tennessee Bar Association Press.
Book production by Gina Lage.
Illustrations by Dave Jendras.

Additional copies of this book may be ordered
from the publisher by calling 1-800-899-6993.
$10.00. Add $2.00 for postage and handling.

ISBN: 0-9701286-0-6

For the Honorable Claudia Swafford Haltom

I *love you*, Your Honor

Many of these works are reprinted from *The Tennessee Bar Journal* and the *Tennessee Young Lawyers Quarterly*, with permission.

Illustrations by Dave Jendras
Front cover: Caricature of Bill Haltom with Perry Mason & Hamilton Burger on TV.
Section I: Bill as TV judge on *Hollywood Squares*.
Section II: Bill's first kiss.
Section III: Casual Day in the courtroom.
Section IV: Ed McMahon in courtroom being questioned about $11 million payout.
Section V: Modern day Creationist monkey trial.
Section VI: Jerry Falwell and his lawyer celebrating a touchdown in the end zone.
Section VII: Sam Ervin, Howard Baker, Richard Nixon.
Page 114: Allie Prescott.

Introduction

My first meeting with "Billy" Haltom was memorable. I was a 19-year-old orientation assistant at the University of Tennessee. My job was to make soon-to-be freshmen feel at home on their one-night tour of college. Naturally, when I looked across the courtyard and saw a scrawny little guy with a very young face playing basketball all alone, I immediately assumed he was a freshman. I went out to make him feel less lonely. I was mortified to learn that he was not only much older than me, but was the president of the student body. Billy immediately cracked a joke, which made me feel much less humiliated. I quickly learned that his sense of humor is one of the things that makes him so special.

I also learned the hard way that same summer how helpful that sense of humor could be. On the night that the campus police stopped us rolling down Cumberland Avenue in a laundry cart, his quick question of, "Oh, officer, were we speeding?" certainly diffused what could otherwise have been a fairly tense situation.

Over the years, I have seen that sense of humor develop. Even after he grew up, became "Bill" instead of "Billy" and became a lawyer, a husband and a father, he maintained his sense of humor.

God knows that being a father and a husband requires a sense of humor, but you may be surprised to know that many lawyers have a sense of humor. It may be because lawyers have to find a way to deal with so many bad lawyer jokes. It may be because lawyers simply need a way to deal with the stress of conflict in the everyday practice. Either way, a lot of lawyers can tell funny stories.

What is surprising and refreshing about Bill Haltom's sense of humor is that you can share his stories and jokes with anyone — even your mother. His stories do not rely on four letter words to get a laugh. He is subtle and sweet, and his stories will tug at your heart.

Another fascinating aspect of Bill's stories is that even though they are often about lawyers or lawyer-related topics, they do not appeal just to lawyers. His stories touch everyone by reminding them of something that meant a lot when they were children — things as simple as a little league baseball game or that moment of wonder when we all sat transfixed as John Glenn circled the earth the first time.

Bill's stories focus on families and the things that are important to families. He reminds you of the days when we saw the world through a black-and-white TV screen and the good guys actually won.

He also reminds us of another well-kept secret about lawyers. They really do stupid things sometimes. His blunt, but funny, analysis of cases such as the O.J. trial are entertaining as well as illuminating.

Finally, you should know that Bill is really a good guy. Not only will he keep you entertained with this book, but he has agreed to donate all of the proceeds to the Tennessee Legal Community Foundation, a non-profit organization dedicated to furthering the ideals of professionalism in the practice of law and providing education about and access to the legal system. By buying this book, you are not only guaranteed a good time, you are also supporting a good cause.

Pamela L. Reeves
Tennessee Bar Association President 1998-1999

Acknowledgments & Preface

Nearly 20 years and three kids ago, I got a phone call from my dear friend Pam Reeves. She asked if I would write a "legal humor column" (as opposed, I guess, to an *illegal* humor column) for the *Tennessee Young Lawyers Quarterly*. I told her that in my opinion, "legal humor" was an oxymoron like "jumbo shrimp," "student athlete," or the official oxymoron of the American Bar Association, "working vacation."

Nevertheless, I agreed to give it a try. I then spent the decade of the '80s trying to be funny four times a year.

And then in 1990, having "aged out" of the Young Lawyers Division, I became an old geezer humor columnist for the *Tennessee Bar Journal*, requiring me to try to be funny once a month.

Well, if you spend two decades trying to be funny four to twelve times a year, you'll eventually have a book on your hands, or more accurately, in *your* hands.

Since we lawyers are always looking for somebody to blame when things go wrong, who shall we find liable for this book?

Well, I plead guilty. But I have a lot of co-conspirators who should each be assessed some degree of comparative fault. For starters, there is Pam "Laundry Cart" Reeves, of course. And she is followed by a host of volunteers including Charles "Big Screen TV" Swanson, Lucian "Excuse Me!" Pera, Don "I'm Part of the Vast Right Wing Conspiracy" Paine, Sarah "Trixie" Sheppeard, Johnny "Ain't No Mountain High Enough" Tarpley, Randy "Nolo Contendere" Noel, Katie "Life-On-The" Edge, Suzanne "How Do We Know This Isn't Trash?" Robertson, Gary "Fast Ball" Hengstler, Anne "Blonde Ambition" Fritz, "Air Ed" Townsend, Allan "I Once Appeared on the Cuzin' Tuny Show" Ramsaur, Gina "When Can We Expect Your Column, Mr. Haltom?" Lage, Cissy "Just Put the Money on the Table" Daughtrey, Gil "Air Conditioning" Campbell, Howard "The Reasonable Man" Vogel, Barbara "I Gave Up

My Maiden Name for the Name Mayden" Mayden, The Right Reverend Roy Herron, Buck "Where's the Stadium At?" Lewis, and, of course, the fabulous Joni Prouser.

Fault should also be attributed to my partners at the firm of Thomason and Hendrix, who certainly could have put a stop to all this years ago had they only had the foresight to tell me to quit writing and go back to work.

I won't ask that you assess liability on my buddy Dave Jendras. As you will see, his illustrations are terrific and the columns that accompany them aren't his fault.

Finally, liability in this case should also be imposed on the judge … specifically, the most beautiful lawyer ever to put on a pair of black robes, the Honorable Claudia Swafford Haltom.

So was I right when I told Pam that "legal humor" was an oxymoron? For your sake, I hope not.

In any event, I await your verdict.

Bill Haltom

Contents

SECTION 1

*I'm Not a Lawyer,
But I'll Play One on TV*

In Search of Hamilton Burger

When I was a little boy growing up in Frayser, Tennessee, I didn't know any lawyers. There were no lawyers in my family. My father, my uncles, and all the other men in our family were preachers. My mother, my grandmother, my aunts, and all the women in my family were June Cleaver-type full-time mommies. And none of the other moms and dads in my neighborhood were lawyers.

But although there were no lawyers in my family or in my neighborhood, I did know two lawyers, even though I never met either one.

The first was a brilliant trial lawyer named Perry Mason. He came into my life when I was five years old and he appeared in black and white on the TV set in my family's living room. As a boy growing up in the Eisenhower era of the late 1950s and in the New Frontier of the early 1960s, I was in awe of this man. Indeed, I wanted to grow up to be just like him.

Perry was a phenomenal lawyer who had two incredible attributes. First, he always represented innocent people. Second, he always won.

And Perry didn't just win. He won big. You see Perry was a criminal defense lawyer who did not believe in the reasonable doubt defense. He didn't do this weenie Johnnie Cochran stuff of "if it doesn't fit you must acquit." The way Perry won a case was that he did what O.J. is now doing, only he did it successfully. He always found the real killer. The way he proved his client was innocent was by finding the real killer and bringing him to justice.

Moreover, Perry would expose the real killer right in the courtroom during the trial. That's because for reasons I still can't figure out, whenever Perry was defending a case, the real killer attended the trial, and would be sitting in the audience in the courtroom.

Now if I ever murdered someone — and this is a hypothetical I'm dealing with — and someone else was accused of the crime, I guarantee you the last place I would show up would be the trial. I mean if I'm the real killer and some poor innocent schmuck gets framed and is being defended by F. Lee Bailey in the Shelby County Criminal Court, I guaran-dog-gone-tee-you I ain't gonna be there to watch it.

But when Perry was defending a case, the real killer always came to the trial and sat in the courtroom, I guess just to make sure he got away with it.

And then, Perry would win his case through a dramatic cross-examination. Now Perry Mason was the greatest cross-examiner in the history of the American legal system. His cross-examination was so effective it not only affected the witness on the stand, it affected everyone in the courtroom, especially the real killer. As Perry would wear down the witness on the stand through his cross-examination technique, he would also wear down the real killer, so that eventually Perry's cross-examination would be interrupted. The real killer would jump up from the gallery and yell, "Stop it, Mr. Mason! Stop it! He didn't kill him, I did!"

It was an awesome performance.

The second lawyer I got to know when I was a little boy was a man by the name of Hamilton Burger. Hamilton was the ill-fated prosecutor on *The Perry Mason Show*. Poor Hamilton Burger had the longest losing streak in the history of American jurisprudence. He lost one nationally-televised trial each week to Perry from September of 1957 through May of 1966, a total of 36 losses per year for a grand total of 360 consecutive defeats. It was as if the defense team of Perry, Della, and Paul Drake were the Florida Gators and poor Hamilton Burger was the Tennessee Volunteers.

To this day, Hamilton continues to lose case after case after case to Perry as the reruns continue in syndication. Indeed, at this very moment, somewhere in America, somebody is watching Hamilton lose once again to Perry Mason.

Now when I was little boy, I wanted more than anything to grow up to be a lawyer just like Perry. I wanted to always represent innocent parties, and I wanted to win every time I walked into a courtroom. But I've now practiced law for over 20 years. I have a wife, three kids, a dog and a cat, a minivan and an adjustable rate mortgage. And I can tell you, folks: Perry is no longer my hero. My hero, indeed my role model as a lawyer, is Hamilton Burger.

So why, you ask, has Hamilton Burger become my hero? Simple. Here is a man who lost one case a week in a nationally-televised jury trial to Perry Mason for over 10 years, and yet he never lost his job as district attorney. Think about that. Hamilton must have more political clout than Bill Clinton, Ken Starr, and Jesse "The Body" Ventura combined.

The older I get, the more I admire Hamilton Burger. Any man who lost as often as he did and yet continued to pursue his life's calling as a prosecutor, must have been a man with real character.

It was awfully easy for Perry Mason to be a lawyer. It was easy to win week after week after week after week. I would imagine that Perry never had trouble keeping the spirits up back at the office. Perry's office probably never had a bad Christmas party. And when you win week after week after week, you never have to give a pep talk to Paul Drake and Della Street.

But think of the character, the sheer tenacity and the Churchillian spirit ("Never give in!") that Hamilton Burger had to show as he went back to trial week after week after week only to lose time and time and time again, as if he were the starting point guard for the Washington Generals. When you think about it, you can only reach one of two conclusions about Hamilton Burger. Either he was a really stupid man who could not figure out anything else to do in life but let Perry Mason beat him every week, or he saw himself as part of a process, a process of the pursuit of justice. And part of his role in that pursuit of justice was to go after Perry's clients until Perry exposed the real killer.

Contrary to public opinion, Hamilton Burger was no loser. In fact, he was a much better prosecutor than Gil Garcetti. The citizens of Los Angeles County were very well-served by Hamilton Burger. The crime rate in Los Angeles no doubt stayed low during Hamilton's years as prosecutor, because real killers never went free. Thanks to the combination of Hamilton Burger as prosecutor and Perry Mason as defense lawyer, the innocent were always vindicated and the guilty always went to jail.

So here's some unsolicited advice for my fellow trial lawyers: We all need heros. If the only clients you have in your practice are innocent people who never did a thing wrong in their life, your hero should be Perry.

But if you're like me, and if from time to time you've actually represented someone who's made some mistakes in life, you can find inspiration from the man who truly was the most inspirational trial lawyer of all time: not the undefeated Perry Mason, but the always-defeated but-always-perseverant Hamilton Burger, a lawyer who lost 360 consecutive nationally-televised trials and never lost his job.

•••

Why Didn't They Televise the Three Stooges Trial?

On behalf of millions of sophisticated, intelligent television viewers, I have a question for the executives of the major networks: Why didn't you televise the Three Stooges trial?

For several years during the decade of the '90s, every time I turned on my television, I was forced to watch news broadcasts concerning the O.J. Simpson legal proceedings. Twenty-four hours a day, seven days a week, we were treated to non-stop coverage of the *State of California v. O.J.*, starring Johnnie Cochran, Marcia Clark, F. Lee Bailey, and Jerry Mathers as the Beaver.

Believe it or not, I saw a segment of *The Today Show* in which Bryant Gumbel and Katie Couric actually discussed the topic, "Is the media giving too much coverage to the O.J. Simpson trial?" This was a little like *The National Enquirer* featuring the headline: "Are We Giving Too Much Coverage to Elvis Sightings?"

I'm surprised the cable TV company didn't bring us the "O.J. Channel" or "O.J. Span" for those Americans who want continuing coverage of the O.J. Simpson legal proceedings uninterrupted by such trivial matters as international news developments, economic reports, the NBA playoffs, and The Psychic Friends Hotline.

For the life of me, I can't understand how one criminal trial, even with a celebrity defendant, merits extensive television coverage previously reserved for truly important events such as Mid-East Wars, Olympic Games, earthquakes, *Who Wants to Be a Millionaire* or "Celebrity Week" on *Jeopardy*!

What makes this even more baffling is that the networks gave us non-stop broadcasts of the O.J. Simpson legal proceedings while totally ignoring truly important jury trials, such as the case of *Curly and Larry v. Moe*.

As all educated Americans know, Curly, Larry and Moe comprised the Three Stooges comedy team. For nearly 50 years, the Stooges gave America a very sophisticated, dry form of comedy that consisted primarily of poking each other in the eyes and hitting each other on the heads with sledge hammers.

When I was a little boy, I was a big fan of the Stooges and their subtle, understated brand of humor.

Therefore, I was extremely interested to read in the newspaper that the heirs of Curly and Larry had sued the heirs of Moe, claiming that Moe had cheated Curly and Larry out of merchandising profits. (Interestingly enough, Shimp was not a party.) The trial of the case was completed, and the jury slapped (so to speak) Moe's daughter and grandson for a $3 million verdict in favor of Curly's widow and Larry's grandkids.

I wish the TV networks had broadcast this trial. I guarantee you that I and millions of other Three Stooges fans would have watched every minute.

First, I would like to have watched the jury selection. If O.J. Simpson can't get a fair trial, there's no way in the world Moe could get a fair trial. Every one of us who has ever watched a Three Stooges film can tell you that Moe was the "intelligent Stooge" (relatively speaking) who always duped Curly and Larry. For example, it was Moe who was always poking Curly and Larry in the eyes and hitting them over their heads with sledge hammers.

Whenever Curly or Larry tried to retaliate and poke Moe in his eyes, Moe would always cleverly stop their fingers by holding his hand across the bridge of his nose. Having thwarted such efforts, Moe would then look condescendingly at Curly and Larry and say, "Nyuk! Nyuk! Nyuk!"

Now I ask you: Who among us could have given Moe a fair trial? We all know he always mistreated Curly and Larry. Perry Mason couldn't have won a verdict for Moe.

Moreover, I would love to have watched the Three Stooges trial on television when the jury verdict came in.

I'll bet Curly and Larry's lawyers poked Moe's lawyers in their eyes. And then, for good measure, Curly and Larry's grandkids looked at Moe's kids and said, "Nyuk! Nyuk! Nyuk!"

•••

I'm Not a Judge, But I'll Play One on TV!

I've recently decided it is time for a career change. I don't have a new job lined up just yet. But I know what I want to do. I want to be a judge. But I don't want to be just an ordinary judge. I want to be a Hollywood judge.

I don't want to spend a career in a courtroom. I want to spend it in a TV studio!

I don't want judicial chambers! I want a dressing room!

And I don't want a law clerk! I want an agent!

When I was a little boy there was only one Hollywood judge. He was Judge Hardy, Mickey Rooney's daddy in the old Andy Hardy films.

Judge Hardy was always dispensing fatherly judicial wisdom to Andy and to Andy's girlfriend, Judy Garland.

But other than Judge Hardy, there were no Hollywood judges. For example, I can't recall who played the judge in any of Perry Mason's trials against Hamilton Burger.

But these days Hollywood is full of judges. Indeed, the biggest stars on TV these days aren't cowboys or cops or even lawyers. They are judges!

For starters, there is Judge Judy, who should not be confused with Officer Judy from the old *Smothers Brothers* TV show.

Judge Judy is such a mega-star that she not only hosts her own show (entitled, surprisingly enough, *Judge Judy*), but she is also one of the stars regularly featured on *The Hollywood Squares*. As all good couch potatoes know, *The Hollywood Squares* is a very popular quiz show featuring contestants so dumb they don't even have to answer the questions. Rather, the questions are answered by Hollywood superstars who sit in cubicles on a giant Tic-Tac-Toe board.

Well, Judge Judy is such a big star that she sits right up there on *The Hollywood Squares* Tic-Tac-Toe board right between Whoopie Goldberg and Charro. And the dumb contestants say things like, "I'll go to Judge Judy to block!"

Now you show me a judge who is a star on *The Hollywood Squares*, and I'll show you a truly powerful judge. You never see Sandra Day O'Connor or Ruth Bader Ginsburg on *The Hollywood Squares*.

Judge Judy not only stars in two TV shows. She's also married to Judge Sheindlin, the star of *The People's Court*. You read that right, microwave popcorn breath! Judge Judy and Judge Sheindlin of *The People's Court* are a real life married couple. They are the Lucy and Ricky of Hollywood judges.

In addition to Judge Judy and her Hollywood judge husband, there is also Judge Joseph Wapner, a judge with higher name recognition than Chief Justice Rehnquist. For many years Judge Wapner presided over *The People's Court*, although he has never been married to Judge Judy. But now Judge Wapner is the host of *Judge Wapner's Animal Court*, a TV show featuring lawsuits between household pets. It's sort of *Lassie* meets *Court TV*.

If you grow tired of watching dogs and cats fight on *Judge Wapner's Animal Court*, you can always change the channel over to *Judge Mills Lane*, starring surprisingly enough, Judge Mills Lane! Judge Lane is such a big-time star that he also referees heavyweight championship boxing matches. So help me, it was Judge Lane who disqualified Mike Tyson for biting off a piece of Evander Holyfield's ear. Hey, folks, that's entertainment!

And then, of course, there is my fellow Memphian, Judge Joe Brown. He is the star of a TV show called (believe it or not) *Judge Joe Brown*.

Judge Joe Brown is the biggest TV star to come out of Memphis since Cybill Shepherd. He's not exactly Judge Elvis, but he is a big star.

Well I'm not a judge, but I'm sure ready to play one on TV! I say it's time for the *Judge Bill Show* starring ... ME! With the lovely Vanna White as my courtroom clerk and Doug Lewelyn as my bailiff as I preside over the case of *Lassie v. Rin Tin Tin*.

And my ultimate dream is that someday when I'm the biggest Hollywood judicial star of all, I'll be sitting right up there in that center square, with Whoopie Goldberg to my left and Charro to my right. And a really dumb contestant will whisper those magic words: "I'll go to Judge Bill to block!"

•••

Thank Goodness L.A. Law *was Cancelled*

My fellow lawyers, thanks to the Good Lord above and declining Nielsen ratings below, the NBC television network cancelled L.A. Law. After eight seasons of giving our profession a bad name, Arnie Becker and the law firm of McKenzie & Brackman (a group that would never be mistaken for Perry Mason, Paul Drake, and Della Street) have faded from our TV screens.

I say good riddance. That's because the L.A. Law TV series was one of the worst things that ever happened to the legal profession. L.A. Law did for us lawyers what Dallas did for oil "bidnessmen," what The Andy Griffith Show did for deputy sheriffs, and what Gilligan's Island did for cruise navigators. In short, it made us look like a bunch of turkeys.

I honestly believe that during those eight years, the L.A. Law TV series hurt the legal profession in three significant ways.

First, L.A. Law contributed to the continuing decline in public esteem for our profession. How did L.A. Law hurt the image of lawyers? Simple. Any lay person who saw a single episode of L.A. Law would be convinced that every lawyer in America does two things: first, he or she collects millions of dollars in legal fees. Second, when not collecting millions of dollars in legal fees, he or she is having an affair with either (a) a client, (b) a law partner, (c) an associate, (d) a secretary, (e) a judge or (f) all of the above.

That's clearly the image projected by the "star" of L.A. Law, a ruthless loverboy named Arnie Becker.

A typical one-hour episode of L.A. Law went like this: In the first half hour, Arnie would win a multi-million dollar jury verdict. Then, after a brief commercial break, Arnie would spend the second half hour sleeping with the jury that just gave him the big verdict. When Arnie wasn't flashing his briefs in either the courtroom or the bedroom, viewers of L.A. Law got to watch a long-running affair between a male and female partner of McKenzie & Brackman. I can't remember the male lawyer's name, but I definitely remember that the female lawyer was Susan Dey, an actress who 20 years ago distinguished herself by starring in a television show called *The Partridge Family*.

Well, I'm sorry, folks, but I could never take Susan Dey seriously in her portrayal as a lawyer. Every time she appeared in a courtroom scene, I kept expecting her to lead the court and jury in singing a rousing chorus of "C'mon, Get Happy."

I kept hoping she would call David Cassidy as a witness so he could sing, "I Think I Love You!"

Or perhaps she would load up the entire McKenzie Brackman law firm in a paisley bus.

The second way that L.A. *Law* hurt lawyers is that it convinced millions of college students to go to law school, thereby contributing to the glut in the profession. Believe it or not, applications to law schools in America increased dramatically several years ago at about the same time that L.A. *Law* hit the top of the Nielsen rating charts. Fortunately, as the show's ratings declined, the number of applications to law school started dropping as well.

Coincidence? I think not. Some 30 years ago when NBC cancelled *Bonanza*, there was a similar drop in the number of college students who decided to pursue careers as cowboys. Moreover, there have been very few family singing groups in America since *The Partridge Family* was cancelled, not coincidentally, during the last days of the Nixon administration.

Finally, L.A. *Law* hurt the legal profession because it convinced an entire generation of new lawyers in America that if you want to be a good lawyer, you've got to act like a jerk. Every successful lawyer on L.A. *Law* acted as if they were J.R. Ewing with a law license.

If you watched an episode of L.A. *Law*, you would get the very distinct impression that the Hollywood Bar Association has not issued guidelines for professional courtesy. On L.A. *Law*, if Arnie Becker was not making love to another lawyer, he was probably threatening or slugging her.

Once I was in a deposition with a young lawyer who ranted, raved, threatened me with sanctions, and generally behaved like my youngest child does when she hasn't had an afternoon nap.

After a while, I asked him, "By any chance did you ever watch L.A. Law?"

"Sure," he snarled back.

I wasn't surprised. I was just thankful that he didn't try to have an affair with me.

No doubt about it, thanks to L.A. Law, our profession is plagued by a hoard of Arnie Becker wannabes.

And so the next time I'm sitting in my recliner enjoying an evening of cable surfing, I will definitely not cry in my microwave popcorn over the fact that I can no longer watch L.A. Law.

Frankly, I'm looking forward to watching the new NBC series Chicago Accounting. It will be the compelling story of a bunch of mean, ruthless CPAs who recklessly audit their clients and then make love to them.

•••

Court TV? *Not When I Can Watch the Gorgeous Ladies of Wrestling*

I realize that most lawyers spend their evenings reading advance sheets, treatises such as White and Summer's *Textbook on the Uniform Commercial Code*, or the pocket parts of *Corpus Juris Secundum*. However, I confess that I generally spend my evenings watching cable TV.

Each night, with the help of man's best friend (the automatic channel changer), I simultaneously watch CNN, ESPN, MTV, the Larry King Show, and re-runs of *Green Acres*, starring that renowned lawyer, Oliver Wendell Douglass, and Arnold Ziffle, the world's smartest pig. I've been known to watch some of these shows for as long as three or four seconds at a time.

During one evening of channel surfing, I discovered that there is a cable TV network called *Court TV*. This channel features televised jury trials 24 hours a day, 7 days a week.

Well, folks, I'm a trial lawyer (not a litigator, mind you, since I actually see the inside of a courtroom on a regular basis). As such, I spend about 60 to 70 hours a week either in court or preparing to go to court.

Accordingly, when I go home at night, the last thing I want to do is sit back in my recliner and watch a jury trial such as the *State of Florida v. Manuel Noriega*, with play-by-play by Keith Jackson and color commentary by Nina Totenberg (Jackson: "Oh, my goodness! That Hillary Shrumbaker is some kind of prosecutor!" Totenberg: "Right, Keith, but you'll notice on the instant replay that she asked one question too many during that last cross-examination!")

I admit that from time to time I have watched legal proceedings on TV. For example, several years ago, I watched the trial of Teddy Kennedy's nephew on CNN, primarily because I wanted to see if Uncle Teddy would be called as a character witness. (Kennedy: "Yes, I served as my nephew Willie's chaperone on spring break.")

But instead of Uncle Teddy, all I saw was a witness with a big blue bubble over her face.

I also spent the entire month of September 1991, watching the televised hearings on the confirmation of U.S. Supreme Court Justice Clarence Thomas. The heavyweight championship fight between Judge Thomas and Professor Anita Hill was the legal equivalent of the televised tennis match I watched 30 years ago between Billie Jean King and Bobby Riggs.

But otherwise, I have never regarded televised legal proceedings as compelling entertainment.

If you give me a choice between watching ESPN's Celebrity Mud Wrestling or watching a televised jury trial, I'm going to opt for mud wrestling every time, particularly if it involves really big celebrities like Vanna White or Pat Sajak.

Now I ask you: Would you rather watch Lawrence Tribe debate Robert Bork on PBS's *That Delicate Balance* or watch a loser-leave-town World Wrestling Federation grudge match between Michael Jackson and Lisa Marie Presley?

I realize that the law is a jealous mistress, but hey, babe, lemme put my feet up and watch a little *Monday Night Football*, okay?

After all, I've spent the entire day deposing an expert witness who charges $250 an hour to talk about asbestos. Give me a break! Let me watch *Jackpot Bowling* or *Andy of Mayberry*.

You say public broadcasting has a special on the life of Clarence Darrow? Well, maybe some other time. Right now I'm watching the Gorgeous Ladies of Wrestling heavyweight championship bout between Linda Tripp and Monica Lewinsky.

•••

O.J. Simpson, Esquire

Y ou may remember O.J. Simpson. He was on TV and in the newspapers all the time before Monica Lewinsky came along.

Well, in case you are wondering whatever happened to O.J., here's a bulletin: He's studying to become a lawyer.

You read that right. According to several news reports, O.J. Simpson has interrupted his endless "pursuit of the real killer" to take law school courses by correspondence.

Faster than you can say, "If it doesn't fit you must acquit," O.J. Simpson may soon become America's newest lawyer.

Think about this. O.J. Simpson, Esquire. This is just what the legal profession needs. Like Bill Clinton would need another White House intern to call Ken Starr.

The irony is that O.J., who used to be an actor, is trying to become a lawyer just as all the real lawyers in his life are leaving the legal profession to enter show business.

Chris Darden, the prosecutor who tried to send O.J. to prison, starred in *One Hot Summer Night*, an ABC made-for-TV movie about a murder involving a professional athlete who has a blonde trophy wife. Wonder how they came up with the plot?

O.J.'s defense counsel, Johnnie Cochran, has hosted his own cable TV show, featuring his trademark iambic pentameter poetry. ("If you turn on your TV, you're gonna see me!")

Judge Lance Ito, who played the part of Hop Sing in a remake of the TV series, *Bonanza*, is considering leaving the bench to star in his own one-man Broadway show, *Lance Ito Tonight!*

Meanwhile, Alan Dershowitz will soon leave the faculty of Harvard Law School, as he and Justice Sandra Day O'Connor will replace Pat Sajak and Vanna White as hosts of TV's *Wheel of Fortune*.

Well, I'm not surprised that so many lawyers are going into show business. After all, at one time or another virtually every lawyer in America has dreamed of being either Gregory Peck or Raymond Burr.

However, for the life of me, I can't figure out why O.J. Simpson wants to give up his promising career in *Naked Gun* movies to become a lawyer. Maybe he figures his vast experience in criminal and civil cases has given him a unique ability to help other innocent victims of police conspiracies.

Or maybe after all he's been through, he thinks being a criminal defense lawyer is a pretty easy job. All you have to do is wear a nice suit and come up with a word that rhymes with "DNA."

But the most startling news of all is not that O.J. Simpson wants to be a lawyer or even that Chris Darden would star in a made-for-TV movie called *The Kato Kaelin Story*. No, the really big news will come later when Marcia Clark announces that this fall she's going to be a running back for the Buffalo Bills.

•••

Coming Soon: Torts R Us or The Law Firm That Represents Only Innocent People

Not so long ago, law firms had pretty boring names such as Dewey, Cheatem & Howe, or Engulf & Devour, or Bewitched, Bothered & Bewildered.

But thanks to some innovative lawyers in Memphis, law firms across Tennessee may soon have exciting names.

Believe it or not, I recently received a letter from a Memphis law firm that calls itself, "The Medical Negligence Law Firm."

According to its letterhead, The Medical Negligence Law Firm is a firm that limits its practice to medical negligence claims.

Since I defend a lot of medical malpractice cases in my practice, I am tempted to rename my firm, "The Law Firm That Represents Only Innocent Doctors Who Always Comply With the Standard of Care."

That would certainly make for an impressive introduction to the jury during my next trial. Judge Ito would look at the jury and say, "Representing the defendant is Mr. Bill Haltom of The Law Firm That Represents Only Innocent Doctors Who Always Comply With the Standard of Care!"

I don't do any criminal defense work, but I guarantee you if I did, I would strongly consider renaming my firm, "The Reasonable Doubt Law Firm" or "The Law Firm That Represents Innocent Defendants Who Never Should Have Been Indicted in the First Place."

Perhaps I could call it, "The If It Doesn't Fit, You Must Acquit Law Firm."

Any day now, we will probably turn on our television and see an ad that goes something like this:

> Hi friends! I'm J. Cheever Loophole of The Law Firm That Represents People Injured by Heavily Insured Defendants! Remember, friends; our practice is limited

to the representation of people who are injured by heavily insured defendants, so if you're a person who was injured by a heavily insured defendant, give us a call! Our operators are standing by!

A few years ago, my friend Barbara Mayden wrote an article for the *Memphis Bar Association Magazine*, in which she predicted that a law firm would someday try to market itself under the name "Torts R Us." I thought it was a funny line when I read it, but it turns out Barbara was a prophet. Not only will we soon have law firms called Torts R Us, but we will probably also have Sam's Wholesale Law Club, Wal-Law, Mid America Law Factory Outlet, and Circuit Court City, where service is state of the art.

How about the McLawfirm? Just look for the golden gavels.

Twenty years ago the U.S. Supreme Court ruled that lawyers had a First Amendment right to advertise. Before the Supreme Court issued that decision, the only lawyers you ever saw on TV were Perry Mason and Hamilton Burger. But these days, every time you turn on the boob tube, lawyers appear on the screen, hawking their legal business as if they were selling laxatives, corn soles or hemorrhoid medication.

Law firm ads have become so slick that many firms have hired professional actors to star in the commercials. I keep expecting one of those actors to say, "I'm not a lawyer, but I play one on TV." In the very near future, I'll probably be cable-surfing late one night, and I'll come across the *Psychic Lawyers Hotline*. Your host Dionne Warwick will interview members of The Law Firm of Psychic Lawyers Who Know All About Your Case Without Even Asking You a Single Question!

After watching this for a few seconds, I'll zap the old remote control to the next channel where I will watch *Amazing Legal Discoveries*, an hour-long infomercial starring members of The Law Firm That Always Settles Cases with Amazing Results!

And then I'll zap the old remote control channel changer one more time, so that I can switch to Channel 147 and watch *America's Funniest Video Depositions*, sponsored by The Law Firm of Lawyers Who Really Care About People and not Banks or Corporations.

Or perhaps I'll switch over to channel 132 and watch Mutual of Omaha's *Wild Litigation Kingdom*. I'll watch footage of an accident while the host says, "Jim distracts the unsuspecting accident victim, while I attempt to settle the case by shooting the accident victim with my tranquilizer gun!"

Well, I'd really like to keep watching all these infomercials and other law firm-sponsored TV shows, but I really don't have time. I've got to head to a partnership meeting. I'm going to suggest that we change the name of our firm to "Law Mart." If you're ever sitting in the lobby of our law firm, you may hear the receptionist announce on the P.A. system, "Attention Law-Mart Shoppers!"

•••

SECTION II

Is it True Blonde Lawyers Have More Fun?

The Two Things Every Lawyer Needs to be a Success

My law partner, General Al Harvey, once said that a lawyer needs two things in order to be a success: grey hair and hemorrhoids. You need the grey hair to make you look distinguished and the hemorrhoids to make you look concerned.

Measured by this standard, I may soon be the most successful lawyer since Perry Mason. Off the top of my head, I have to say I've achieved at least half the ingredients for a successful law career. My hair is getting whiter every day.

Years ago there was a television commercial that posed the powerful and intriguing theological question: Is it true blondes have more fun? Well, unless I purchase a lifetime supply of industrial strength Grecian Formula, I'll soon know the answer to that question.

Over the past several years as my hair has turned progressively whiter, I've reassured myself that when I turn completely grey, I'll look like Phil Donahue. Unfortunately, as it turns out, I'm looking more and more like Newt Gingrich every day.

It's too late to take the Grecian Formula route. My wife and kids and friends and co-workers have observed my head for years now, and have watched the slow, steady transformation of my mane from Midnight Black to Old Geezer Grey. I can't exactly just put some liquid shoe polish on my hair tonight as if I were Richard "The Fugitive" Kimble trying to escape from Inspector Girard.

Why if I showed up for work tomorrow with jet black hair, my co-workers would decide that I was either crazy or had applied for a new identity under the Federal Witness Relocation Act, as if I were the good guy in a John Grisham novel.

Until recently, I was fairly despondent about my grey hair. I even considered signing up for a recovery program for greying baby boomers. ("My name is Bill, and my hair is white.")

But then the other day, something wonderful happened. No, my hair didn't start turning darker, nor did somebody tell me I looked like Phil Donahue.

I was reading a copy of *Time* magazine when I came across a stunning color photograph of my favorite actress, Elizabeth Taylor. Now I've been a fan of Elizabeth Taylor ever since she starred in *National Velvet*. If you're old enough to remember Elizabeth Taylor in *National Velvet*, your hair is definitely white.

I've been a fan of Elizabeth Taylor's for so long that I can remember when she married Richard Burton the *first* time.

Having been a fan of Liz for nearly a half century, I was surprised to see her recent photo in *Time*. Yes, there was the star of *National Velvet*, *Cleopatra* and *Who's Afraid of Virginia Woolf*, with completely grey hair. And do you know what? She looked fantastic! Why if I weren't already happily married, I'd be honored to be her eighth husband. Of course, as the old joke goes, I'd know what to do, I just wouldn't know how to make it interesting for Liz.

Well, the Silver Liz has changed my whole attitude about grey hair. Even if I tried to dye my hair, I seriously doubt that Liz or my wife or any other woman would mistake me for a young Eddie Fisher singing "Oh my Grey Papa."

Thanks to the Silver Liz, I'm gonna quit worrying about my hair and start enjoying my new life as a blonde. If grey hair is good enough for Cleopatra, it's good enough for me.

•••

Terms of Endearment: I Love You, Your Honor, or Honey, May it Please the Court!

Recently the Memphis Bar Association published *Guidelines for Bias-Free Conduct*, a brochure outlining how we lawyers should address one another in politically-correct, gender-neutral terms.

Part of the brochure counsels members of the Memphis Bar Association to avoid addressing another lawyer with "terms of endearment and diminutive terms" such as "honey, sweetie, dear" or "little lady, pretty girl, or young lady."

While the document does not specifically say so, we can safely assume that the following terms of endearment should also be avoided:

Sugar Babe

Apple Dumplin'

Precious

Princess

Babe, as in, "My lawyer is a real babe," or "That judge is a babe."

Now, before I go any further I must confess that I am a gender-specific writer. Specifically, I'm a life-long member of the male gender and proud of it. Those rumors about my previous career on the women's professional tennis circuit are completely untrue.

Also, I strive to be a "sensitive male" just like Alan Alda and Phil Donahue or our gender-sensitive president, Bill Clinton, who throughout his career strived for bias-free conduct. For example, during his years as governor of Arkansas, and later as president, Mr. Clinton always chased women, never babes.

As a sensitive member of my gender who is striving for enlightenment, I support the basic concepts of the *Guidelines for Bias-Free Conduct*. I had better. My wife would kill me if I didn't.

However, I have two basic problems with the *Guidelines* as written.

First, the *Guidelines* list terms that male lawyers should avoid using in referring to female lawyers. However, the *Guidelines* do not list terms that female lawyers should avoid using in being gender-sensitive to men. For example, the *Guidelines* should also counsel female lawyers to avoid the following terms of endearment in addressing male lawyers:

> Beefcake
> Stud Muffin
> Hunka-Hunka Burning Love
> Tripod
> Honey Buns
> Big Dog
> Elvis

The other problem I have with the *Guidelines* is that they do not deal with the sensitive issue of how a lawyer of one gender should address a lawyer of another gender when the lawyer of the first gender is married to the lawyer of the second gender. This is not a hypothetical situation. For the past 19 years, I have been happily married to a lawyer of the other gender. She's not only a lawyer, she's a judge.

Every night for the nearly 20 years, upon my arrival at home, I have always shouted out (and I hope this doesn't offend anybody):

"Honey, I'm home!"

"Honey" is a term of endearment I use in reference to the lawyer of the other gender with whom I share three kids, a house, two cars, a dog, a cat and an adjustable mortgage. (We have retained our separate identities and toothbrushes.)

Moreover, I have to admit that over the years I have often addressed the lawyer of the opposite gender to whom I am married by using one or more of the following terms of endearment:

> Sweetie Pie
> Sugar Lips

Doll
Darling

There are some other terms of endearment that I have used over the years, but I will not share them with you inasmuch as I do not wish to embarrass the lawyer of the other gender with whom I share the three kids, the house, the cars, the dog, the cat and the mortgage.

I realize that a liberal construction of the *Guidelines* could lead one to conclude that "terms of endearment" should be avoided only in the professional or legal business context. That is to say, it is not necessary in the privacy of my own home for me to say to my wife, "I love you, Your Honor." Nevertheless, a fellow can't be too sure in this day and age, so I'm not taking any chances. When I get home tonight I'm going to say, "May it please the Court! I'm home, Your Honor!"

•••

Let's Make a Divorce Deal!

Like most baby boomers, I grew up watching TV game shows. Before I even started elementary school, I learned an awful lot about life by watching Eisenhower-era TV quiz shows such as *The $64,000 Question*, *The Price is Right*, *Truth or Consequences* and *Queen for a Day* (which, by the way, had nothing whatsoever to do with the contestants' sexual preferences).

When I was in high school, I became a big fan of the original *Jeopardy!* quiz show, starring the immortal Art Fleming and announcer Don Pardo.

I learned a lot more by playing hooky and watching *Jeopardy* than I ever learned in high school. In fact, thanks to Professor Art Fleming, I became particularly knowledgeable concerning such subjects as State Capitals, The Roaring '20s, U.S. Presidents, Inventions, PotPourri, and Odds and Ends.

In fact, I used to fantasize about appearing on *Jeopardy* and having triumphant moments in Final Jeopardy, such as the following:

Art Fleming: And now we move to our champion, Bill! He has written, "Who was Ferdinand Magellan?" IS RIGHT! And how much did he wager? … All $10,000! And Bill is still our undefeated champion!

Studio Audience: Cheers wildly!

Me: (Humbly) Thanks, Art. I'll be back tomorrow.

Also, when I was in high school and college, I learned a lot about romance by watching a quiz show called *The Dating Game*, hosted by the sophisticated and urbane Jim Lang. The contestants were cool bachelors who dressed like Hugh Heffner and posed intriguing questions to "bachelorettes." "Bachelorette Number 1, if you were a fruit, what kind of fruit would you be?" The bachelorettes would coo back their answers

("A luscious peach!") and then the really cool bachelor contestant would select a bachelorette to take with him on an all-expense paid, chaperoned date!

When I was in college, I used to watch a particularly inane TV game show called *Let's Make a Deal*, starring "TV's Top Trader, America's most beloved game show host, Monty Hall!"

The studio audience on *Let's Make a Deal* featured (in the announcer's words) "… These people, dressed as they are!" Most of the studio audience resembled contestants in a Boy George Look-Alike Contest, and these people (dressed as they were) would jump up and down and scream, "Monty! Monty! Monty!"

Monty would offer contestants a chance to trade in a Cuisinart or a Waterpik for whatever was behind Door Number 1, Door Number 2 or Door Number 3.

At the end of the show, one lucky member of the audience would win the Big Deal of the Day, like a 1975 Chrysler Cordoba with real Corinthian leather, of course.

As a member of the *Leave It to Beaver* generation, I learned an awful lot growing up watching TV quiz shows. However, until recently, I thought that most of what I had learned would be helpful only when I played "Trivial Pursuit" or tried to call the "Trivia Hotline" on a local radio station.

But I've now discovered some wonderful news: All those years I spent watching Bob Barker, and Monty Hall and Hugh Downs, will soon give me a leg up in my future work as a lawyer. You see, believe it or not my fellow lawyers, TV quiz shows may soon become the newest method of alternative dispute resolution in our legal system.

I read a newspaper article about a new TV game show in England called *Divorce Me!* On this show, actual divorce litigants agree to resolve their cases by competing on a televised quiz show rather than in a courtroom.

Given the popularity of such daytime TV shows as *The People's Court*, *Divorce Court*, and *The O.J. Simpson Show*, there is no doubt in my mind that shows such as *Divorce Me!* will soon become standard fare on American television and the newest means of dispute resolution.

Faster than you can say "Monty! Monty! Monty!," litigants will soon be resolving their disputes on nationally-televised shows such as *Let's Make a Settlement*, *The Verdict is Right* or *Truth or Nonsuit*.

Probate disputes will be resolved by Pat Sajak and Vanna White on *Will of Fortune*. Personal injury cases will no longer be resolved in courtrooms. Instead, the litigants will appear in "this studio filled with glamorous merchandise."

And Judge Monty Hall will submit a case to a studio audience described as "these jurors, dressed as they are!"

Instead of making final argument, plaintiffs' lawyers will wager their clients' damages on the Final Jeopardy answer.

Given these interesting developments in the field of dispute resolution, I'm thankful I spent so much of my youth watching quiz shows. I'll know how to advise my client when Judge Monty Hall asks me if we want to turn in our verdict for what's behind Door Number 2.

•••

Here's Hoping the Statute of Limitations Has Run on My First Kiss

I vividly remember my first kiss. It occurred 38 years ago on an autumn day in 1958 in the cloakroom of Mrs. McMurtry's second grade class.

I was seven years old and hopelessly in love with a classmate named Kathy. She was an auburn-haired beauty who was the Julia Roberts of our second grade class.

For several weeks I had tried desperately to get Kathy's attention. During lunchtime I would sit next to her in the school cafeteria, hoping that she and I could share a romantic mid-day dinner by candlelight. I would open my Roy Rogers lunch box, pull out my thermos bottle with the picture of Roy and Dale and Trigger on the side, and offer Kathy my favorite dessert, a Hostess Twinkie®.

At recess, I would try to catch Kathy's eye during the kickball game, secretly dedicating each kick to my true love.

I even wrote Kathy a love letter, a missive scribbled with one of those huge pencils on tablet paper that featured dotted lines to separate the capital and lower case letters.

Kathy responded to my efforts by doing precisely what women have always done when they want to drive a man crazy. She ignored me. She snubbed me as if I were Ross Perot and she were a member of the Presidential Debate Commission.

Of course, this just made me more hopelessly in love with her.

I then tried to win her heart by making her laugh. I would cross my eyes for her or try to regale her by doing my imitation of the Three Stooges. "Nyuk! Nyuk! Nyuk!"

Kathy never laughed. She never even smiled. She obviously did not share my appreciation of the Three Stooges's dry, understated sense of humor.

And then one morning it happened. I found myself in the cloakroom with Kathy, as we were both removing our canary-yellow school raincoats. I caught a glimpse of Kathy's green eyes, and before I knew it, I just walked up to her and gave her a big juicy kiss, right on the lips. It wasn't just some little wimpy kiss like Prince Charles gave Princess Diana on their wedding day. Nosireebob. I kissed Kathy as if she were Scarlett O'Hara and I were Rhett Butler.

I thought a lot about that first kiss when I read the news reports about the six-year-old boy in Lexington, N.C., and the seven-year-old boy in New York City who were accused by school bureaucrats of sexual harassment for kissing female classmates.

I guess I'm pretty darn lucky that it's been 41 years since that first kiss. Although I haven't confirmed this with either Johnnie Cochran or Perry Mason, I believe the statute of limitations has run on any sexual harassment suit Kathy might file against me. No, Kathy never sued me for sexual harassment for that first kiss. She never told Mrs. McMurtry about it, so no school bureaucrat kicked me out of school.

But on that autumn day in 1958, Kathy did something far more powerful than filing a sexual harassment suit or turning me over to school authorities for discipline. What she did was this: shortly after I had given her the big juicy on her lips, Kathy returned the favor by making direct contact with my lips, only she did it with her fist. That's right. Kathy responded to my kiss by giving me a big knuckle sandwich to enjoy along with my Twinkie for lunch that day.

Yes, sweet little Kathy, that delicate flower of Southern womanhood, decked me as if she were Muhammad Ali and I were Barney Fife. And as I picked myself up off the cloakroom floor, I was more in love with her than ever.

I have no idea where Kathy is now. But I'll tell you one thing. I've never gotten over that woman.

•••

In Louisiana, When You Say "I Do," You'd Better Mean It

Nineteen years ago, I played a very small role in my wife's wedding. I was the groom. I had only one line in the entire production, and it was a very short line at that. On cue, I said, "I do!"

Actually, I had a few other lines, but they just involved repeating what the preacher said, as if I were a large tape recorder dressed in a tuxedo.

But if my wife and I ever decide to renew our wedding vows in the State of Louisiana, our next wedding ceremony could get pretty complicated. That's because Louisiana has put some teeth in wedding vows.

The governor of Louisiana signed into law a new classification of marriage in the Pelican State, the so-called "covenant marriage."

A covenant marriage is tougher to get into than your typical forsaking-all-others-till-death-do-us-part marriage. Before a couple can get a license for a covenant marriage, they must go through pre-marital counseling, as if they are about to get into something serious. And once you say, "I do!" in a covenant marriage, you'd better be prepared to stick with the contract. That's because under the new law, a couple in a covenant marriage will only be able to get a divorce by proving physical or sexual abuse, abandonment, adultery or cruelty. There will be no such thing as a no-fault, quickie divorce in a covenant marriage.

Let's face it. A covenant marriage is not the sort of thing Elizabeth Taylor ought to sign up for.

The proponents of the "covenant marriage" idea see it as a panacea to our divorce culture. Last year there were more than one million divorces in the United States, and nearly half of the couples in America who pledge to forsake all others end up hiring a divorce lawyer.

These days wedding vows are sort of like a politician's campaign promise, or the warranty on a new car. After a while, we throw the rascals out and elect a new politician. The car warranty expires, and it's time for a trade-in.

We live in an era of trophy wives. After the kids are grown and the wife has, say, about 100,000 miles on her, a successful businessman buys her out and purchases a sleek new model. Of course, now that so many women are executives and successful business people, we middle-aged men may soon find ourselves the victim of trophy husbands, as our wives trade us in for some guy in his twenties with a flat stomach.

But now, at least in the state of Louisiana, some husbands and wives may actually be held to their wedding vows. Some guy will stand before a preacher and look his bride in the eyes and promise to stay with her "till death do us part." These words will be interpreted in the state of Louisiana as containing an actual promise that the man will stay with his wife for the rest of his or her life. Imagine that.

And then the bride will look at her husband and promise him that she will stay by his side "for better or worse, richer or poorer, in sickness and in health." As a partner in a covenant marriage, she will actually be required to keep this ridiculous promise by sharing a life with her husband even when the going gets tough.

And then, when the same couple look at each other and promise "to forsake all others," this will actually be interpreted to be a promise they will be faithful and committed to one another.

Well, this covenant marriage idea will never work. It is totally contrary to all modern notions of marriage. Those Louisiana lawmakers are just hopelessly out of touch with the times. They think when a fellow makes a promise to his wife, he's supposed to keep it. Imagine that.

•••

SECTION III

*No Lawyer Ever Said on his Death Bed,
"My One Regret is That I Did Not
Spend More Time at the Office"*

Casual Day: A Bad Idea Whose Time Should Not Have Come

For many years my friend Richard Day ran the best men's clothing store in downtown Memphis. The store, appropriately named "Richard's," was the place for downtown "bidnessmen" who wanted to put their best wing-tipped or tasseled-loafered foot forward. From the days when the well-dressed Ronald Reagan was president to the closing years of the 20th century, Richard's Men's Store was the place to go in downtown Memphis for conservative suits, pinpoint cotton shirts and silk ties.

But in 1998, Richard Day closed the doors of his store forever. The reason? Two words: Casual Days.

Somewhere in America sometime during the last several years, some unkempt lawyer or businessman in a wrinkled suit came up with a truly bad idea. He decided that one day each work week would be designated "Casual Day" so that he and his employees could show up for work in so-called "casual clothes."

Suddenly "Casual Day" spread through the American legal and business community like a bad soup stain. All across America people started showing up for work on "Casual Day" (generally Friday) dressed in blue jeans and tee shirts emblazoned with silly little slogans such as "Accountants never lose their balance" or "Lawyers do it in their briefs."

All of this was bad enough, but faster than you could say "body odor," Casual Day suddenly spread like fashion kudzu to not just one day but several days a week. These days lawyers, bankers, CPAs, and even funeral directors often show up for work wearing golf shirts, khaki trousers, and penny loafers.

If this trend continues, when you consult with your CPA next winter, you may find that your income tax return is being prepared by someone wearing a tank top, Madras shorts and flip-flops. And when this happens, I think you will agree with me that Casual Day stinks. Literally.

My well-dressed friend, Richard, is absolutely convinced that Casual Day did in his business. "Men just aren't wearing business suits anymore," Richard explained to me. "And worse yet, not only do they look unprofessional, they are proud of it!"

Well, my friend Richard is not the only one suffering from this dramatic decline in the sartorial standards of American lawyers and businessmen. We're all paying a price for Casual Day.

Everywhere I go these days, men are looking more and more like slobs. When I go to church on Sunday morning, other men appear in the congregation dressed as if they were headed for the golf course. And I'm not talking about Pebble Beach. I'm talking about a goofy golf course.

When I take my wife out to dinner at a nice restaurant, I often notice that sitting at the table right next to me is some guy wearing a baseball cap. And he's wearing it indoors, for crying out loud. It's bad enough that a guy goes out to dinner wearing a John Deere tractor hat, but didn't this guy's momma teach him when he was a boy that a man takes his hat off when he goes inside?

And perhaps worst of all, whenever I get on an airplane for a "bidness trip," I almost always find myself sitting next to some guy the size of a Japanese Sumo wrestler who's wearing a tank top and cut-off shorts. So help me, I believe that there is an inverse relationship in America these days between obesity and the amount of clothing worn. That is to say, the fatter the guy is who is sitting next to me on an airplane, the more likely it is that he will be wearing virtually nothing at all.

The Casual Day phenomenon has had a particularly bad effect on the legal profession. Now we lawyers know how we should dress for work. Men-type lawyers should wear dark pin-striped suits, white shirts, silk ties and wing-tips ("Air Nixons"). Female-type lawyers should wear dark suits, white blouses and wing pumps ("Air Renos"). But to put it bluntly, many lawyers are showing up for work these days looking about as goofy as Johnnie Cochran did when he put on O.J.'s knit cap.

For example, I recently attended a deposition in which opposing counsel was wearing (so help me) a Hawaiian print shirt. Suffice to say that this guy did not have a physique that could qualify him for the cast of *Baywatch*. He looked like a cross between the Goodyear Blimp and Don Ho. I kept expecting the guy to pull out a ukulele and start singing "Tiny Bubbles."

On another recent occasion, I showed up at the Shelby County Circuit Court for a hearing on a petition to approve a workers' compensation settlement agreement, where I was greeted by my adversary, a *pro se* plaintiff who was wearing shorts, a tee shirt and sneakers. The guy looked like he was headed for a vacation on the Redneck Riviera.

Our judge was the Hon. Karen Williams, who, I might add, was dressed from neck to wing pumps in a beautifully tailored set of black robes.

Judge Williams, bless her conservative heart, is a woman of high sartorial standards. Believe me, she does not allow Casual Day in Division III of the Shelby County Circuit.

So she told my adversary that she would not hear his petition until he put on a pair of long trousers or otherwise covered his legs. Well, so help me, the guy borrowed a raincoat, and put it on to cover his naked legs. We were then allowed to proceed with the hearing. So there I was, sitting at the hearing in my pin-striped suit and wing tips, looking like Dick Nixon, while my adversary was sitting next to me in a raincoat. Throughout the entire hearing, I was scared to death that the guy was going to flash the judge.

Well, I believe it was the immortal and well-dressed Victor Hugo who once wrote, "Stronger than the body odor of the largest army is a bad idea whose time has come."

Casual Day is a bad idea whose time should never have come. So I implore you, my fellow American lawyers. You may not care how you

look, but I and a lot of other men in coats and ties and women in dress-
es sure do. So please dress up a little before you head to your church or
your office. And especially before you sit next to me on an airplane.

•••

Tasseled Loafers? No! ...
Cowboy Boots, Wing Tips, Pumps, Yes!

There's something I've been wanting to get off my chest, or more accurately, my feet. I would like to put to rest, once and for all, this ridiculous notion that we lawyers wear tasseled loafers.

Recently lawyer-bashers have attacked what they mistakenly believe is the foundation of America's lawyers: tasseled loafers.

This nonsense about lawyers' footwear began at the 1992 Republican National Convention when, in his acceptance speech, President George Herbert Walker Bush thoughtfully blamed America's problems on "sharp lawyers who wear tasseled loafers."

That's right, my fellow Americans. Everything bad that has happened to this country in recent years (Hurricane Andrew, the $4 trillion debt, Michael Jackson, your brother-in-law, etc.) has all been caused by us well-heeled lawyers who stomp around America in our tasseled loafers.

I'm not quite sure what kind of shoes Mr. Bush wears. Since he is a Texan from Connecticut whose home is in Maine, he probably wears Brooks Brothers L.L. Bean cowboy boots.

But even though Hillary defeated George in the '92 elections, all this malarkey about lawyers in tasseled loafers continues unabated. I heard a national commentator say that President Clinton's medical malpractice tort reform proposals will "no doubt be vigorously opposed by the tasseled loafer crowd!"

Well my fellow sole brothers and sisters, let's stamp out this tasseled loafer myth once and for all.

Now if the shoe fits, we lawyers will wear it. But the truth of the matter is that virtually no lawyer in America ever wears tasseled loafers, except when playing golf.

Lord knows you never see a lawyer in court wearing tasseled

loafers. Did you ever see a single episode of Perry Mason in which Perry (God rest his soles) wore a pair of tasseled loafers? I once saw Paul Drake wearing a pair of Guccis, but private investigators have always been a jazzier crowd.

No, the truth of the matter is that lawyers in America wear three types of shoes: cowboy boots, wing tips or navy blue pumps. Plaintiff's lawyers generally wear cowboy boots. That's because your typical plaintiff's lawyer fancies himself as either Wyatt Earp or the Marlboro Man. Yessireebob, he's a-gonna ride into the courtroom and shoot up some of them thar bad guys from the insurance companies.

Hey! Who was that masked man with the silver briefcase? Hi-yo, Contingency Fee! Away!

Defense lawyers generally wear ugly black wing tips, the official shoe of the American Bar Association. Ugly black wing tips are sometimes referred to as Air Nixons, since Dick Nixon popularized wing tips during his presidency 30 years ago. I can still remember those photographs of President Nixon walking the beaches of San Clemente in his wing tips. Now there was a defense lawyer on vacation!

Increasingly, of course, the footwear of choice for America's lawyers are navy blue pumps. After all, the attorney general of the United States is one tough woman but I doubt if she's going to feel comfortable in either cowboy boots or high-heeled wing tips.

And according to the National Public Radio's Nina Totenberg, Sandra Day O'Connor never wears tasseled loafers under her black robes.

So beware lawyer-bashers! We lawyers are gonna start kicking back … with either our pointed heels or our size-13 triple D wing tips!

•••

The Three Worst Inventions of All Time

I don't mean to be, in the words of a former vice president, a nattering nabob of negativism. But, in the words of a former president, let me make one thing perfectly clear: I believe that fax machines, cellular phones, and personal computers are the three worst inventions in the history of American technology.

Virtually every lawyer in America now has all three diabolical devices, and these machines are threatening to enslave us.

There have been some pretty dark days in my life, but by far the worst was the day my office got a fax machine. I haven't had a moment of peace since.

Twenty-four hours a day, 365 days a year, fax machines across America spit out endless pages of "urgent" letters and documents. 99.99% of these letters and documents are not urgent at all. But when the fax machine spits them out, we must stop everything we are doing and immediately examine the fax letter or document as if it were something truly magnificent such as the Rosetta Stone or the winning entry in the Publisher's Clearinghouse Sweepstakes or the outline of John Grisham's next novel.

In those innocent days prior to the advent of the fax machine, most lawyers led pretty organized lives. We could come into our offices each morning, get ourselves a good cup of coffee, and then sit down at our desk and go through the morning mail. That mission accomplished, we could then spend the rest of our day as Elvis used to say, taking care of bidness.

But with the fax machine, it's absolutely impossible for us to have any kind of organized day. The fax machine says jump, and we immediately ask, "How high?"

When we're not swapping faxes, the odds are we're using that second diabolical device — the cellular telephone.

Thanks to cellular phones, you and I will not have one moment of peace and quiet until the roll is called up yonder and we're there. Thanks to cellular phones, we are now accessible not only when we're in the office, but when we are in our cars, on airplanes, in bass fishing boats, at football games, in the bedroom and in the bathroom. We've all become like LBJ who used to conduct important matters of presidential business while sitting in the presidential john.

On those rare, wonderful moments when we are away from a phone, many of us have little pagers strapped to our waists, so that we can be "beeped" for one of those urgent messages we get about 700 times each day. Thanks to pagers, we're all becoming more and more like doctors, who for years have walked around constantly beeping, as if they were all crickets rubbing their hind legs together.

When we're not faxing each other or calling each other from our cars, or beeping like Roadrunner, we're probably working on our personal computers.

The painful truth is that most lawyers these days spend more time with their personal computer than they spend with their families. We've got our desktop computers in our offices and little laptop computers that we tote around with us all the time so that we will never be without our good little buddy, Mr. Computer. It's as if we're the Skipper, and our laptop is Gilligan (or maybe it's the other way around).

Every time I get on a commercial airflight these days, I can't help getting the feeling that I've walked back into my old high school typing class. Both the first class and coach cabins are always filled with bidness people who are typing away on the keyboards of their personal computers. Sky King meets Rosemary Woods.

These days, Mr. Computer even goes with us on vacation. Years from now, our children will remember those wonderful summer vacations to the beach. It was so much fun building sandcastles, collecting seashells, and chasing waves while Mommy or Daddy sat in a lounge chair, pounding away on the old laptop computer.

"Surfs up, everybody! Wait a minute! You're getting suntan lotion on my modem!"

These days I hear more and more business folk complain of being tired. Well, as my two sons, Wally and Beaver Haltom, are fond of saying, "Duh!"

Is it any wonder that we're all tired when we go through life constantly being faxed, phoned, beeped and downloaded?

I think it's time you and I turn off the fax machines, take the phone off the hook, and look for the exit ramp on the information superhighway.

I say it's time for an honest-to-goodness vacation without Mr. Laptop. I say it's time for a long nap on a Sunday afternoon.

Okay, let's do it. Unfortunately, I can't right now. My secretary just handed me a fax.

•••

Memo to Associates: We Do Not Allow the Consumption of Microwave Popcorn or Moon Pies in the Office

Hey, Mr. and Ms. Lawyer! Before you take another bite of that Twinkie® you're munching, you'd better check your firm's office manual. You may be violating official firm snack policy.

According to an article in a recent edition of *The Compleat Lawyer* (which should not be confused with *The Incompleat Lawyer*, *The Intercepted Lawyer* or *The Pass Interference Lawyer*), many large law firms across the country have official policies governing the consumption of food and beverages in the office.

For example, if you are an attorney with the firm of Jenner & Block in Washington, D.C., you are not allowed to eat popcorn in your office. That's right, Orville Redenbacher-breath. Those fun-loving, denture-wearing partners at Jenner & Block have banned popcorn consumption in the office since "it makes the office smell like a carnival."

Presumably, hungry lawyers at Jenner & Block are allowed to munch on other smell-free snacks such as Raisinettes®, Goobers®, SnoCaps®, and Goo Goo Clusters®, which are, by the way, the official snack food of the Nashville Bar Association.

While the snack food policies of Jenner & Block sound pretty repressive, it could be worse. Again, according to *The Compleat Lawyer*, the law firm of White & Case in New York City allows "in-house eating only in the firm's cafeteria." You read that right, corn pup breath. White & Case is so fancy it has its own Morrison's right in the offices.

To my knowledge, there is not a single law firm in the state of Tennessee that has an in-house cafeteria. However, I do know several outstanding law firms that are located within walking distance of a Cracker Barrel Restaurant.

In Atlanta's King & Spalding, lawyers can apparently enjoy snacks on the premises. However, according to *The Compleat Lawyer*, a King &

Spalding lawyer had better not let Griffin Bell catch her drinking a Pepsi-Cola® in the office. Since the firm represents Coca-Cola® (or as we pronounce it in the south, "co-cola"), the partnership does not exactly regard Pepsi as "the right one, baby, uh-huh."

Thirsty lawyers in the Washington, D.C., firm of Squire & Sanders are allowed to sip coffee and other beverages only if they agree to use an official law firm regulation lidded mug. According to *The Compleat Lawyer*, Squire & Sanders presents all new employees with regulation lidded mugs. The firm has also issued an official policy prohibiting "the carrying of beverages through the corridors in open containers." Similar lid rules are enforced in the New York firm of Fried, Frank, Harris, Schriver & Jacobsen, and in the Chicago firm of Ross & Hardies.

I can just see some poor young associate wandering down the hallowed halls of Squire & Sanders on his first day on the job.

"Hold it right there, young Mr. Hungadunga!" roars senior partner Thurston B. Howell III. "Is that an open, unlidded cup of coffee you are carrying down the hall? Haven't you read Section 162(b)(4)(a)(ii) of the office manual?! Don't you realize that you were about to spill your Starbeans caffe latte mocha cappuccino all over the firm's tasteful oriental rugs?"

Well, I just hope that the stuffed shirts on my firm's executive committee don't get wind of this. Faster than you can say "Moon Pie," they'll knock out some high-falutin' memo announcing that pizza deliverymen, Twinkies®, Dunkin Donuts®, Yoo-Hoo® chocolate drinks, and Hostess Ding Dongs® are henceforth banned from the premises.

Call me old-fashioned, but I wouldn't turn in my Twinkie even if my partners gave me an official lidded coffee cup with the firm logo emblazoned on the side.

I don't care if my partners open an in-house restaurant called "La Maison D'Bon Appetit D'Billable Hours." I want to exercise my Constitutional right to eat a pepperoni pizza right at my desk.

As far as I am concerned, we lawyers should be allowed to eat and drink anything we want to within the privacy of our offices so long as we don't burp out loud when we come out.

•••

Voice Mail: What We Have Here is Something Worse Than a Failure to Communicate

One of the great moments in American history occurred in 1876, when Alexander Graham Bell made the first telephone call. As an astonished crowd watched, Bell phoned his assistant, Thomas A. Watson, and uttered those immortal words, "Watson, come here. I want you."

Few people know that in response to his words, Alexander Graham Bell heard the following recorded message:

> Hi! This is Watson. I can't come to the phone now, but when you hear the beep …

It could have been worse. Bell could have heard the following message:

> You have reached the offices of Watson. If you know the first four letters of Watson's last name, push the pound button and then enter your Social Security Number. To access the Watson Company directory, press "star" and then enter the square root of the year of your birthdate …

One of the great ironies of our time is that as communication technology continues to advance, we Americans are no longer able to talk to each other. Our phone system has become so complicated that instead of talking to each other, we just spend most of the time talking to machines.

Once upon a time in America, most people had just one phone. It was a big, black heavy object that weighed about 25 pounds. It looked like a bowling ball with ears. You couldn't carry it around your house or your office without getting a hernia. You couldn't put it in your car or talk into it while you walked down the street. You had no alternative but to attach yourself to it and stand or sit right beside it when you used it.

But nowadays, virtually everyone in America is walking around with a little telephone hooked to the sides of their ears. Business people are regular communications cowboys as they walk around with telephones in holsters, strapped to their waists, as if they were Wyatt Earp, Marshal Dillon or Palladin. "Have phone will travel."

Millions of Americans walk around with pagers strapped to their belts, causing them to constantly beep and chirp like crickets.

Now you would think that this proliferation of cell phones and beepers would mean that we Americans would now be talking to one another like a bunch of magpies. But nothing could be further from the truth.

The great American philosopher, Yogi Berra, once commented on a Manhattan restaurant by stating, "It's so crowded, nobody ever goes there anymore."

By the same token, we Americans now have so many phones and beepers that we never talk to each other anymore. Instead, we just constantly leave messages on each other's machines.

For example, a few years ago, if I wanted to call my friend, Bubba, I just picked up the heavy ears off my bowling ball telephone and then dialed Bubba's number on a little rotary wheel. If Bubba was home, he answered the phone by saying, "Yello!" or "Yo!" or "It's your nickel, so start talkin'!"

Nowadays, when I call Bubba, I hear the following message:

> You have reached the residence of Bubba and Wanda McGillicuddy and their two precious children, Bubba Jr. and Sissy, and Wanda's mama, Bertha. Bubba and Wanda and Bubba Jr. and Sissy and Bertha can't come to the phone right now, which means they may not be here, and then again, maybe they are here, so don't try to break in and rob them because they have a very hungry Doberman Pincher who loves to eat burglars. Your

phone call is very important to Bubba and Wanda and Bubba Jr. and Sissy and Bertha, so when you hear the beep, please leave your name, the date and time of your call, your phone number and a detailed message. Thank you … B-E-E-P!

By the end of this lengthy recorded message, I have forgotten just why in the Sam Hill I called Bubba in the first place. Moreover, even if I have the energy to leave Bubba a message, this doesn't mean that Bubba and I will ever talk. When he returns my call, he will simply have to leave a message with my machine. Of course, he could reach me on my beeper, in which case I'll just beep him back.

If communications technology continues to advance, the day will soon come when Bubba and I have absolutely no contact whatsoever with one another. Our machines will just call each other from time to time and leave recorded messages, and occasionally Bubba and I will beep out loud for no apparent reason.

Well, to paraphrase a line from that classic film, *Cool Hand Luke*, what we have here is something a heckuva lot worse than a failure to communicate.

•••

SECTION IV

The Write Stuff

It was a Dark and Stormy Lawsuit

My fellow lawyers, here is some news that can make us all proud. For the second consecutive year, a lawyer has won the nation's top award for bad writing.

David Hirsch, a 47-year-old public defender in Seattle, was recently named the recipient of the 1999 Bulwer-Lytton Purple Prose Award. This coveted award is named in honor of the 19th century British novelist, Edward Bulwer-Lytton, who once began a book with the immortal words, "It was a dark and stormy night."

The Bulwer-Lytton Purple Prose Award is the Heisman Trophy of lousy writing. For over 20 years, the award has been given annually in recognition of the worst opening sentence of a novel. Traditionally, lawyers have dominated this competition, proving beyond all doubt that we lawyers are the worst writers in America.

Mr. Hirsch's winning entry in this year's Bulwer-Lytton Purple Prose competition truly met the low standards of non-creative writing by lawyers. Here in its breathtaking entirety is Mr. Hirsch's award-winning prose:

> Rain, violent torrents of it, rain like fetid water from a god-sized pot of pasta strained through a sky-wide colander, rain as no one knew it, flaming the shuttering trees, whipping the white-capped waters, violating the sodden firmament, purging purity and filth alike from the land, rain without mercy, without surcease, incontinent rain, turning to intermittent showers overnight with partial clearing Tuesday.

No doubt about it, when it comes to lousy prose, David Hirsch has the write stuff.

Hirsch modestly credits law school and 20 years of law practice for his ability to write such terrible prose. In a recent interview with the *National Law Journal*, Hirsch said, "I've had an interest in bad writing for many years. Law school put a certain polish on my badness, and 20 years of practice helped."

Amen, Brother Hirsch. No truer words were more poorly written. When it comes to bad writing, no one can hold a pen or a Dictaphone compared to America's lawyers.

We lawyers are truly America's worst writers. No one can match our ability to take a clear, cogent thought and translate it into legal language that one can decipher only with the assistance of the Rosetta Stone.

Twenty-five years ago when I entered law school, I could write simple declarative sentences. Having received an undergraduate degree from the University of Tennessee, I was capable of writing clear and concise sentences such as the following:

> It's football time in Tennessee!
> How about them [sic] Vols?
> Where's the stadium at [sic]?

But during my three dark and stormy years at the University of Tennessee Law School, I was taught not only to think like a lawyer, but to write like one. I was taught to use legal words such as "aforementioned" and "above-referenced" and "hereinafter" and "subsequently."

After I graduated from law school, my writing only got worse. I actually found myself dictating incomprehensible prose such as, "Comes now the affiant, and after being duly sworn, states as follows, and further affiant sayeth not."

Also, as a lawyer, I learned that I should never use a simple word when a longer and more obscure one would do.

For example, when I was just starting out as a lawyer, I would make the mistake of writing a clear sentence such as the following: "After her car wreck, the plaintiff had to go to the hospital."

But after just a few years of law practice, I was able to write the following: "Subsequent to her automobile accident, the plaintiff incurred extensive and permanent disabilities to her body and person, necessitating immediate emergent care."

I also learned that in legal writing it was important to be redundant and to use as many words as possible, cluttering my prose with parenthetical cross-references. For example, I learned to write:

> The party of the first part, (hereinafter referred to as the party of the first part), hereinafter releases, discharges, unties, unbinds, kicks, bites, and tosses away the party of the second part (hereinafter referred to as the party of the second part) from all claims, demands, causes of action, insults, funny looks, politically incorrect jokes, snide remarks, or any claims of any nature whatsoever involving the above-referenced automobile accident and any subsequent emergent and necessary medical care to the body and person of the party of the first part caused in any manner by the actions of the party of the second part, although the party of the second part denies any liability to the party of the first part and denies any responsibility for the above-referenced incident between the party of the first part and the party of the second part and in fact doesn't have a clue as to how this all got started in the aforementioned first place.

Well, after nearly a quarter century of training in the field of bad writing, I believe the time has come for I (or rather me), like the inspirational David Hirsch before me, to scale the Mount Everest of bad prose. Yes, my fellow lawyers, I've decided that subsequent to my aforementioned 25 years of bad writing, the time has come for me to enter the Bulwer-Lytton Purple Prose Contest for the year 2000. Here's my entry for next year's competition:

> It was a dark and stormy lawsuit, the sort of endless litigation that winds and serpentines through years of hearings and depositions and interrogatories and affiants who are duly sworn and deponents who further sayeth not and requests for production of enough bate-stamped documents to threaten the Amazon Rain Forest, until it all culminates with the party of the first part and the party of the second part and their counsel sitting like withering potted plants in a court-ordered mediation session on a long hot August day in an un-air-conditioned courtroom in Henry County.

Well, take that, John Grisham! Eat your heart out, Harper Lee! That was just the first line of my new novel, *The Pelican Boxer Shorts*, soon to be a major motion picture.

And there's plenty more bad prose where that came from.

So call me Ishmael. Call me a cab. But above all, call me and tell me that I'm this year's winner of the Bulwer-Lytton Purple Prose Award.

Further the author writeth not.

The End.

•••

The Secret to Grisham's Success

Recently, I and approximately 10 million other Americans stood in line at my local book store to buy a copy of John Grisham's latest "legal thriller," *The Runaway Jury That Escapes to the Caribbean with Tom Cruise and Julia Roberts*. Grisham is the former Mississippi trial lawyer who has written several best-selling novels including *The Firm*, *The Client*, *The Pelican Brief*, *A Time to Sue*, and my personal favorite, *The Honest Young Lawyer who Beats the Huge Corrupt Law Firm That is Controlled by the Mafia*.

It is an understatement to say that John Grisham is a best-selling author. By last count, Grisham has sold over 54 million books. In fact, Grisham currently ranks second on the list of all-time best-selling authors.

The number one all-time best-selling author is, of course, the Lord, who wrote 66 best sellers including *Genesis*, *Exodus*, *Leviticus* ... well, you know the list.

John Grisham's novels invariably involve the following plot:

1. Innocent poor person who lives in a trailer park is victimized by huge, greedy, multi-national corporation that is controlled by the Mafia.

2. Innocent poor person who lives in a trailer park hires a struggling, poor young lawyer who is the only honest lawyer left in America now that Perry Mason is dead.

3. When poor innocent person who lives in a trailer park and her young, struggling honest lawyer sue the huge, greedy multi-national corporation that is controlled by the Mafia, it hires a huge, greedy, ridiculously expensive law firm to defend the case.

4. In his very first trial ever, the young, struggling, honest lawyer beats the huge, greedy, corrupt defense law firm, winning a verdict for a billion dollars on behalf of the poor person who lives in a trailer park against the huge, greedy, multi-national corporation that is controlled by the Mafia.

5. Angered by losing a billion dollar verdict, the huge, greedy, multi-national corporation that is controlled by the Mafia sets out to kill the young, honest lawyer and the poor, innocent client who lives in a trailer park.

6. Honest young lawyer and poor client who lives in a trailer park secretly take a billion dollars of the Mafia's money, place it in Swiss bank accounts, and then head to a tropical island where they will live forever in paradise with new identities under the Federal Witness Relocation Program.

This basic plot has made John Grisham the all-time winner of the true publisher's clearinghouse sweepstakes, and has made him almost as wealthy as the honest young lawyer becomes at the end of one of Grisham's novels.

So what is the secret of John Grisham's success? Simple, the American public just can't get enough of books, movies, and TV shows about mean, corrupt lawyers.

It's one of the great ironies of our time. According to public opinion polls, lawyers are about as popular as hemorrhoids. Nevertheless, while everyone claims to hate lawyers, the blockbuster movie hits and the highest-rated TV shows are all about mean, ruthless lawyers.

A few years ago, I took my boys, Wally and Beaver Haltom, to the mall cinema to see *Jurassic Park*. I heard the film was about dinosaurs, and I thought it was going to be an animated feature starring Dino Flintstone. But what my boys and I saw that day was not a cartoon. So help me, the highlight of *Jurassic Park* came when a dinosaur plucked a lawyer up from a toilet seat and gobbled him up.

That's right. Little Wally and Beaver and I munched on buttered popcorn while Godzilla munched on a lawyer. Hey, folks, that's entertainment!

Well, the whole thing just made me mad. But I suspect that when John Grisham saw the film, he instantly realized that if millions of people were willing to pay six bucks a piece to see a lawyer get eaten by a dinosaur, they would probably spend twenty-five bucks to read a novel about lawyers attacking each other.

Well, I must go and get back to reading my book. I'm about to get to the part where the honest young lawyer heads for paradise while the Mafia hitman and his lawyer are both eaten by a dinosaur.

•••

They're Gonna Put Me in the Movies

Ever since I was a little boy, I have wanted to be a movie star. Not just any movie star, mind you, but a really big movie star like Tab Hunter, Fred MacMurray, Rin Tin Tin, or Old Yeller.

Virtually every weekend for the past 40 years, I have sat in a mall cinema and munched popcorn or Raisinettes® while watching epic motion pictures such as *Billy Jack and Rambo Meet Godzilla* or *The Texas Chainsaw Proctologist.*

As I've watched Rambo and Billy Jack and Indiana Jones dash across the movie screen, I have thought to myself, "I could do that! If they just gave me a chance, I could be a really big movie star just like Harrison Ford or Benji."

And then one week, I thought my moment had finally arrived. I was sitting in my office, doing the sort of boring work that is done by attorneys who do not appear on L.A. *Law,* when my secretary, Della, told me I had a telephone call.

I picked up the phone and in my best Perry Mason-style voice said, "Yell-oh!"

"Mr. Haltom, this is Jason from casting for *The Firm,*" said the Hollywood-style voice on the other end of the line.

"Say what?" I asked, using the interrogatory form that I learned while growing up in Frayser, Tennessee.

"This is Jason from casting for *The Firm,*" repeated Jason from casting for *The Firm.* "We were wondering if you could be an extra for the film."

For a moment, I was hopelessly confused. I couldn't figure out who this Jason fellow was or why he claimed to be doing fly-fishing for my law firm.

And then (duh!) it hit me. I remembered reading in the newspaper that Paramount Pictures was filming *The Firm* right here in my hometown of Memphis (That's right, folks, Hollywood comes to Hootersville!).

And then my hands began to tremble as I realized that this wasn't just Jason who was calling. This was Hollywood! This was the break I had been waiting for years to get!

"Well," I said in my best Clark Gable-style voice. "What part would I play?"

"You would be an extra," repeated Jason.

"OK," I mumbled, trying to sound like Marlon Brando.

"Fine," said Jason. "Please be at the Mud Island monorail at 6:00 tomorrow morning. We'll be filming a chase scene."

I could hardly sleep on the night before the beginning of my new career as a movie star. I kept wondering what role I would be asked to play in the film. Perhaps I would play a lawyer who is controlled by the Mafia (type-casting). Maybe I would play the part of Tom Cruise's smarter and better-looking brother. Maybe I would be asked to do a love scene with Nicole Kidman or eat oatmeal with Wilford Brimley.

And so the next morning I showed up at the Mud Island parking lot at 6 a.m. for my motion picture debut. After sitting around for nearly four hours, I was called for my big scene. It was then I learned that I had been selected to play one of the most important roles in the film, specifically the part of a man who is walking down a flight of stairs at Mud Island with about 400 other people.

For several hours I stood on a staircase at Mud Island while that world-famous director, Sydney "Tootsie" Pollack shot this highly pivotal scene in which several hundred of us walk up and down a flight of stairs.

I was disappointed to learn that I had no lines. I wanted to say something really dramatic like, "Go ahead make my day!" or "Frankly, my dear, I don't give a damn."

However, all I was ever asked to do was walk down a few steps. Well, as we say in show business, there are no small parts, only small actors.

Unfortunately, it appears that in my first motion picture role I will be not only a small actor, but an itty-bitty, eensy-weensy one at that.

Nevertheless, I'm not discouraged. I predict that I will win the Oscar for Best Supporting Actor Who Plays the Part of a Man Who is Walking Down a Flight of Stairs. And years from now, people will stop me on the streets and say, "Didn't I see you in *The Firm*? You were absolutely great when you and 400 other people came walking down that staircase!"

So move over, Marlon Brando! Step to the side, Clint Eastwood and Sylvester Stallone! At long last, I'm going to be a star!

(Postscript: My big scene wound up on the cutting room floor. In retrospect, I'm glad. Now that I think about it, my nude scene really wasn't relevant to the plot.)

•••

If You Want to be Cool ... Sweat!

Recently my wife and I went to the mall cinema to see A *Time to Kill*, the blockbuster motion picture hit based on a John Grisham novel. The film was typically Grishamesque. A struggling, idealistic young lawyer teamed up with a beautiful, idealistic young law student to comprise the good guy legal team. The bad guy legal team was comprised of a ruthless prosecutor, an unfair judge, and of course, the Ku Klux Klan.

My wife and I munched on buttered popcorn and Raisinettes® as we watched the bad guys burn down the good guy lawyer's house, beat up the idealistic young law student, and do all sorts of other evil things in an effort to thwart justice.

By the time my wife and I had finished eating a tub of buttered popcorn approximately the same size as a large garbage can, the good guy legal team had overcome the forces of evil in a compelling final courtroom scene. That's the great thing about a Grisham movie. Justice always prevails while you eat buttered popcorn.

But as we watched the movie, my wife and I were both distracted by the same point. From the opening scene to the closing credits, every character in A *Time to Kill* constantly sweats. The idealistic good guy young lawyer is always dripping wet, as if he has just stepped out of a sauna. The beautiful young law student glistens with perspiration, as if she spends every spare moment doing the John Grisham-Jane Fonda Home Video Workout (*Sweatin' for Justice*!).

"Why are they all sweating?" my wife asked as she gobbled down another fist full of Raisinettes.

"I don't know," I replied as I chomped on Goobers® and SnoCaps®.

"Maybe the courtrooms in Mississippi aren't air conditioned."

"I never saw Perry Mason sweat like this during one of his trials," observed my wife as she slurped on a giant soft drink approximately the same size as Lake Michigan.

It was only a few days after watching A *Time to Kill* that my wife and I learned why all the characters in the film were constantly perspiring. A young friend of ours who is on the cutting edge of modern trends explained it to us quite simply. These days, it's cool to sweat.

Believe it or not, perspiration is now "in," especially in Hollywood. Superstars like Demi Moore appear on the screen dripping with perspiration as if they are offensive linemen in the middle of two-a-day drills. Megastars Tom Cruise and Harrison Ford appear on the silver screen sweating like Richard Nixon did in the 1960 presidential debate, or like I did during my last IRS audit.

Rock stars and fashion models now sweat like professional wrestlers. During his recent marriage, superstar Dennis Rodman's wedding gown was absolutely soaked.

The news that sweating is now a cool thing to do came as quite a surprise to me. Back in the dark ages when I was young and "with it," I always believed that if you were really cool, you would never sweat. "Don't sweat it," or "No sweat!" were the catch-phrases of the cool of my generation. But now I'm being told that if I really want to be cool like Dennis Rodman or Madonna or Regis Philbin, I need to break out in a cold sweat.

I think I'll go take a sauna. Or better yet, I'll call that IRS agent who did my last audit.

●●●

The Great Escape

Let's be honest, folks. Every lawyer in America spends at least a few minutes each day fantasizing about how to escape from law practice. Yeah, you and I strut around the courthouse or the boardroom wearing dark suits and stern and somber expressions. But just below the worsted wool surface, you and I have a secret life. We long for adventures that have nothing to do with contingency fees, real estate closings, or billable hours.

Let's face it. You and I don't want to be Oliver Wendell Holmes or Felix Frankfurter. We want to be Indiana Jones or Jimmy Buffett.

Unfortunately, however, there are only two ways that a successful lawyer can escape law practice without being committed to a psychiatric institution. The first is to win the grand prize in the Publisher's Clearinghouse Sweepstakes.

The second is to publish a best-selling novel about lawyers who represent the Mafia and are involved in either a gun fight or a sexual encounter every time they go to the office. Well, believe me, I've tried both of these escape plans without success.

For 12 consecutive years I have been a finalist in the Publisher's Clearinghouse Sweepstakes. Each year I get my personal letter from Ed McMahon in which he assures me that I, Mr. William Haltom of Memphis, Tennessee, am about to become an INSTANT MILLIONAIRE!

Ed always says in his letters, "Yes, Mr. William Haltom of Memphis, Tennessee, get ready for your new life as a millionaire because I will soon be announcing on national television that you, Mr. William Haltom of Memphis, Tennessee, have won the grand prize of $11 million payable to, yes, you, Mr. William Haltom of Memphis, Tennessee!"

Each year when I get this personal letter from Ed McMahon, I, Mr. William Haltom of Memphis, Tennessee, immediately start fantasizing about how I will break the news to my law partners that I am retiring at such a tender age.

I've always planned on walking into my firm's weekly partnership meeting and announcing, "Hey, fellas. I want you to meet my good friend, Mr. Ed McMahon of Hollywood, California. Ed has just presented me, Mr. William Haltom, formerly of your law firm, with this check for $11 million, which will not be placed in the firm's trust account, but rather will be placed in the personal account of me, Mr. William Haltom, ex-lawyer, formerly of Memphis, Tennessee, and now of Boca Raton, Florida!"

But despite the fact that Ed keeps sending me these personal letters, the Prize Patrol has yet to come either to my office or my house.

This leaves me with the second escape option, the publication of a truly trashy novel about lawyers.

For the past few months, I have been working on the transcript of *The Naked Law Firm*, which is soon to be both a best-selling novel and a major motion picture. It is the compelling story of young Bradford Remington Tipford III, who graduates number one in his class from Harvard Law School and then turns down a Supreme Court clerkship in order to associate with a law firm in Pigeon Roost, Tennessee, at an annual salary of $275,000 a year plus free use of a luxury John Deere tractor. Young Brad and his voluptuous but innocent wife Mimsy move to Pigeon Roost only to discover that the county law firm of Hungadunga, Hungadunga & McCormick is actually a front for that highly sinister organization, the Future Farmers of America.

And so if Ed McMahon and the Prize Patrol don't come through for me, I'm banking on the success of *The Naked Law Firm*, as well as two other novels I am presently working on: *The Texas Chainsaw Lawyer* and *Billy Jack Sues Rambo*.

Yeah, I'm sure you'll see my name on the best seller list any day now.

In the meantime, you and I had better get back to work.

•••

A Very Personal Letter to Ed McMahon

Mr. Ed McMahon
American Family Publishers
P.O. Box 6200
Hollywood, California

Dear Mr. McMahon:

Ed McMahon of Hollywood, California, you owe millions of dollars in damages! Well, that will be true if the jury returns a multi-million dollar verdict against you and Dick Clark and the American Family Publishers in the lawsuit recently filed against you.

That's right Mr. Ed McMahon, of Hollywood, California! You are already a finalist in the lawsuit claiming that you and Mr. Dick Clark of Hollywood, California, along with American Family Publishers, convinced millions of us to subscribe to all sorts of magazines in the hopes that we might win the grand prize of $11 million in the American Family Publishers Sweepstakes.

That's right, Mr. Ed McMahon, of Hollywood California! For years you have written personal letters to me, Mr. William Haltom of Memphis, Tennessee, telling me that I, Mr. William Haltom of Memphis, Tennessee, am about to win the $11 million grand prize in the American Family Publishers Sweepstakes.

You have also written personal letters to my wife, Mrs. Claudia Haltom of Memphis, Tennessee, telling her that yes, she too is about the win the $11 million grand prize. This has caused a great deal of marital strife in our household, as my wife and I have argued for years over which one of us is going to win the $11 million and how we are going to spend it.

Yes, Mr. Ed McMahon, of Hollywood, California, for years I have subscribed to *Good Housekeeping*, *True Detective Stories*, *Guns & Ammo*, and

Proctology Illustrated in the desperate hope that by subscribing to all of these magazines, I, Mr. William Haltom of Memphis, Tennessee, would soon become "America's newest millionaire!" That's just the way you described me in several personal letters, saying such things as, "William is America's newest millionaire!" Of course you've also used the same words to describe my wife, my father, my Uncle Earl, my Aunt Wanda, and my cocker spaniel, all of whom have subscribed over the years to *Psychology Today*, *Field and Stream*, and *Beekeepers' Digest* so that they too could claim the $11 million, which, after all, they have no right to since the money rightfully belongs to me.

And so, Mr. Ed McMahon, of Hollywood California, you and Dick Clark and American Family Publishers find yourselves as defendants in a civil lawsuit. I hate to tell you this, but your chances of winning that lawsuit are about as good as my chances of becoming "America's newest millionaire." Why? Simple. Every person who will serve on your jury has probably received several personal letters from you telling them they were about to win the $11 million grand prize.

Let's face it, Mr. Ed McMahon, of Hollywood, California. You may already be a loser.

•••

SECTION V

Trials and Tribulations

The Difference Between Trial Lawyers and Litigators

Most kids in America dream of growing up to be a professional athlete, rock musician or movie star.

But when I was a little boy, I dreamed of growing up to be a trial lawyer like Atticus Finch or Perry Mason.

Most little boys growing up in the 1950s dreamed some day of hitting home runs like Mickey Mantle or throwing touchdown passes like Johnny Unitas. But not me. I dreamed that I would grow up to conduct a cross-examination like Raymond Burr or do a closing argument like Gregory Peck.

Let's face it, folks: I was one weird kid.

Well 40 years later, my dream has come true, at least to some extent. No, I can't cross-examine witnesses like Perry, and I don't live next door to Boo Radley. But I am a trial lawyer and proud of it.

However, I've recently noticed that trial lawyers are going the way of the dinosaur. Slowly but surely we are being replaced by a new breed called "litigators."

Litigators claim to try cases, but they really don't. They get cases ready for trial by collecting documents and taking depositions. And they actually go to court from time to time but only to argue motions.

Litigators never do compelling cross-examinations or moving closing arguments for the simple reason that they never go to trial.

Some litigators actually claim to be trial lawyers. But don't be misled.

So how can you tell the difference between a trial lawyer and a litigator? Here's a brief list of the distinctions between the two:

— A trial lawyer worries about witnesses. A litigator worries about documents.

— A trial lawyer hires paralegals and private investigators. A litigator hires litigation support teams.

— A trial lawyer will work on as many as 20 cases during a single week. A litigator will strive to work on only one case during a 20-year period.

— A trial lawyer keeps up with his or her expenses. A litigator always travels first class.

— A trial lawyer is concerned about scheduling a case for trial. A litigator is concerned about scheduling more depositions.

— Trial lawyers generally work on personal injury cases. Litigators work on asbestos cases and class action suits.

— Trial lawyers have been known to give closing arguments in one case and opening statements in another during the course of the same day. Litigators have been known to hold meetings in more than one city during the course of the same day.

— For a trial lawyer, an hour lasts 60 minutes. An hour is shorter for a litigator.

— For relaxation, trial lawyers go fishing. For relaxation, litigators schedule more depositions.

— Trial lawyers don't know how to work copy machines. Litigators operate even the most complex machinery.

— Trial lawyers generally drink whiskey and smoke. Litigators eat apples and drink Perrier.

— There have been many famous trial lawyers including Clarence Darrow, Abraham Lincoln and Daniel Webster. There are no famous litigators.

— Trial lawyers like to recite poetry in closing arguments. Litigators don't make closing arguments.

— Trial lawyers like country music. Litigators like to schedule depositions.

— Hollywood has made many movies about trial lawyers (*Inherit the Wind*, *The Verdict*, and *Adam's Rib*, just to name a few). Hollywood has never made a movie about a litigator.

— Perry Mason was a trial lawyer, not a litigator. Make no mistake about it, Paul Drake and Della Street were not part of a litigation support team.

Well, maybe I'm out of style, but I've decided to try to keep being a trial lawyer rather than a litigator. I'll keep traveling second class. I'll keep worrying about expenses. I'll keep working on 20 cases at the same time. And no matter what the case, I'll always quote Rudyard Kipling in my closing argument.

•••

Monkey Business, The Sequel

Seventy-five years ago, a young high school biology teacher went on trial in a small town courtroom in the mountains of East Tennessee. The teacher was John Scopes, and he was charged with violating a state law that prohibited teaching school children Charles Darwin's theory of evolution.

The "Scopes Trial" became a circus, as a self-righteous, windbag politician named William Jennings Bryant squared off against a flamboyant, arrogant trial lawyer named Clarence Darrow. A cynical journalist named H.L. Mencken covered the trial for millions of readers. Mencken was sort of the *Court* TV of his day.

The Scopes Trial was to the Roaring Twenties what the O.J. Trial was to the Boring Nineties. Judge John T. Raulston (the Lance Ito of his time) quickly lost control of the case, and Bryant and Darrow strutted and preened around the courtroom for the national audience. Just imagine Pat Buchanan and Johnnie Cochran arguing in a nationally-televised trial before a weak judge who never tells them to shut up. That's what the Scopes Trial was like.

It was, of course, just a lot of monkey business. Bryant was pandering to the Religious Right of his day, hoping to jump-start his political career.

Darrow, meanwhile was getting tons of free publicity, sort of like Gerry Spence gets these days by appearing as a legal expert on *The Today Show*. And Mencken, of course, sold newspapers.

Virtually lost in the circus was John Scopes himself who, after all, was simply a substitute teacher who agreed to serve as the political football in this Super Bowl match-up between modern science and old time religion.

It was a sad and sorry spectacle, giving "bad press" to preachers, politicians, lawyers, and people of faith.

Well, brothers and sisters, behold I bring you bad tidings. The monkey business has started back up again, only this time the monkeys aren't found in a courtroom but in the legislature and on school boards.

During a recent session of the Tennessee legislature, state lawmakers debated a proposed law that would ban teaching evolution "as fact" in the public schools. The bill would authorize school boards to fire teachers who violate the law.

Fortunately for Tennesseeans who are at least as smart as chimpanzees, the legislature adjourned without passing the bill. Nevertheless, the bill's supporters have vowed to bring the issue back up during future legislative sessions.

But while the legislature has dropped this monkey business for the time being, the issue has been taken up by a number of school board members across the state who also advocate a dismissal of teachers who teach evolution "as fact."

Well, in the words of Supreme Court Justice Yogi Berra, this is déjà vu all over again. Before you know it, we'll be watching Scopes II or Monkey Business, The Sequel, as another school teacher goes on trial for teaching evolution. The Scopes II Trial will be carried on CNN with expert commentary by Marcia Clark and F. Lee Bailey, assuming Mr. Bailey isn't in jail during the trial.

I can just imagine what the Scopes II trial will be like. Special Prosecutor Pat Buchanan will call Jerry Falwell to the witness stand as an expert in the field of creation science. Defense counsel Johnnie Cochran will claim the teacher's glove doesn't fit. (Hey, it worked before, didn't it?)

Well, Lord please spare us from the great tribulation of Scopes II. The last thing America needs these days is another battle between pandering politicos and cynical lawyers.

I, for one, believe God created the universe. Whether He did it in six 24-hour days, one cosmic explosion, or over the course of millions of years doesn't make a bit of difference to me. The Grand Canyon, a sunrise, and my baby daughter's face are all spectacular examples of God's work, and I'm not one to get bogged down in either the scientific or theological details of how He did it.

The irony is that these politicians are undermining my faith. Watching their antics in the legislature and on school boards has caused me to believe that maybe we did descend from monkeys.

•••

The Trial of Pat Boone

Now that the O.J. civil trial is, thank the Lord, finally over, we can all get ready for the next big nationally-televised trial of a Hollywood celebrity. I'm referring, of course, to the upcoming trial of singer Pat Boone.

No, Pat hasn't been charged with killing anybody. He hasn't even been charged with jaywalking. He hasn't hired Johnnie Cochran or Perry Mason or Matlock or any other lawyer to come to his defense. Nevertheless, Pat is about to stand trial before a very tough jury. The charge against Pat is that he has become a heavy metal, hard rock musician. The jury before which Brother Pat must stand trial is the audience of cable TV's PTL, or *Praise the Lord Show*.

For over 40 years, Pat Boone has been one of the most wholesome entertainers in show business. His image has been so squeaky clean he makes Billy Graham look downright worldly in comparison.

During the 1950s, Brother Pat was the Anti-Elvis, a wholesome, clean-cut boy-next-door, who sang "April Love" and wore white shoes.

Until recently, wholesome Brother Pat entertained millions of faithful fans in a weekly television show, *Gospel America*, carried by cable TV's Trinity Broadcast Network, the same network that broadcast *The Praise the Lord Show*.

But then, Brother Pat did a couple of very strange things. First, he released an album of heavy metal (yes, heavy metal) rock music called "In a Metal Mood/No More Mr. Nice Guy."

And then, Brother Pat appeared on national television, at the American Music Awards ceremony, dressed as a heavy metal rock performer. More specifically, he was bare-chested and wore a leather vest, several tattoos, and so help me, a studded dog collar. He didn't wear his famous white shoes. They don't seem to go well with black leather, tattoos and a dog collar.

The sight of Brother Pat in a dog collar and black leather shocked millions of faithful gospel fans across the country. Suffice to say that gospel music fans were not ready for Snoop Doggy Pat.

Besieged by complaints from faithful viewers from across the country, the Trinity Broadcasting Network cancelled Pat Boone's show and urged viewers to pray for this prodigal heavy metal son.

Which leads us to Brother Pat's upcoming trial. Trinity Broadcasting Network officials believe in redemption, and they've given Brother Pat a plan for his salvation. Brother Pat has been invited to appear on the *Praise the Lord Show* to explain his actions to viewers. Network officials say that if Pat's explanations satisfy PTL viewers, he may be welcomed back to the Trinity Network fold.

Well, brothers and sisters, I had no interest whatsoever in the O.J. civil trial. However, I don't want to miss a minute of Pat Boone's upcoming trial on the PTL show. I can't wait to see what he wears, what he says and what he sings.

Will Prodigal Pat appear wearing his dog collar and black leather or will he go back to his white buck shoes?

Will he sing "April Love" or Guns 'N' Roses?

Will he wear a tattoo that says "Born to Raise Heaven!"?

Will he ask for forgiveness or sing a heavy metal version of "Drop Kick Me Jesus Through the Goalpost of Life?"

This promises to be the best episode of *Praise the Lord* since that memorable day when the studio audience nearly drowned in Tammy Faye's tears and mascara while Jim Bakker was being led off to prison.

(Postscript: Justice prevailed for Brother Pat. Better yet, he won his "PTL Trial" and is now back on the air! Praise the Lord indeed!)

•••

I Do Solemnly Swear That My Testimony Will be Legally Accurate, Although Perhaps Misleading

One of the truly antiquated aspects of our American judicial system is the oath we administer to witnesses during trials. In most courtrooms across America the oath goes something like this: "Do you swear that the testimony that you are about to give will be the truth, the whole truth, and nothing but the truth, so help you God?" In response, the witness generally mumbles something like, "Uh huh" or "Yo" or "You're darn tootin'!" or occasionally, "Say what?"

Throughout American history this hopelessly-old-fashioned oath has been administered to literally millions of witnesses.

But it has become increasingly apparent that this traditional oath is going to have to be amended or modified to conform to our modern society. Let's face it, folks. Asking people to swear not only to the judge and jury but also to the Lord that they will tell not only the truth but the whole truth, for crying out loud, is just something we Americans should no longer be required to do.

There are two basic problems with the old-fashioned truth-the-whole-truth-and-nothing-but-the-truth approach to witnesses. First, it is simply no longer expected or required in American society. With the exception of certain religious fanatics, absolutely nobody these days tells the whole, unvarnished truth. In both our public and private lives, we modern sophisticated Americans have become spin-meisters, responding to any question asked of us by reciting a version of the "truth" that is most favorable to us.

Take for example the president of the United States, William Jefferson Rodham Clinton. Mr. Clinton crossed his fingers, put his left hand on a Bible, raised his right hand in the air, and repeated that old legal mumbo-jumbo about promising to tell the whole truth. And what did the leader of the free world do after stating this oath? Well, by his own admission, he gave "legally accurate" answers followed by public comments that "gave a false impression" and "misled people," including his wife.

While the president says he "deeply regrets" misleading Hillary and the rest of us, he insists he did nothing wrong in simply giving "legally accurate" testimony that "did not volunteer information."

Some religious fanatics and right-wing crazies had the gall to question this Clintonian approach to the truth. But these lunatics who wish to cast stones at our leader are simply overlooking the fact that fibbing has become an American way of life.

From a very early age, we Americans become adept at fibbing at home ("I did not hit my brother!"), and fibbing at school ("The dog ate my homework"). As teenagers, we tell whoppers about how late we got in or where we were or who we were with or what we were doing while we were with them.

By the time we are grown, we Americans are veteran liars. We fib at work. ("I tried to return your call yesterday. Besides I sent you a check last week.") We fib at play. ("Put me down for a 5.") And if the president's legally accurate answers are to be believed (and for that matter, even if they are not), then apparently a lot of Americans even fib to their spouses. They fib on their wedding day by reciting vows that won't keep, and then throughout the course of their marriage, they fib about whether they are keeping their vows. It's just non-stop fibbing from the altar to the divorce court.

No doubt about it, this truth-the-whole-truth-and-nothing-but-the-truth approach to testimony is contrary to our culture and hopelessly out of touch with our lying times.

The second problem with the traditional-but-now-antiquated oath is that it brings a third party into the courtroom, namely the Lord. Why should a witness be required to make a promise to the Lord before testifying? It's bad enough that President Clinton or any other witness might face charges of perjury for "legally accurate" answers that are misleading or convey a "false impression." Should the president or any other witness also have to answer to the Lord for this? Isn't answering to Hillary punishment enough?

And so, my fellow Americans, the time has come for us to face the truth, or rather, to make a more "legally accurate" assessment of what witnesses should have to say before they testify in an American courtroom. Accordingly, although I am not under oath, let me say with all the legal accuracy I can muster, I believe the oath administered to witnesses should be modernized to meet the lower standards of our times for truthfulness and veracity. From now on all a witness should have to say before testifying are the following words: "I hereby swear that my testimony will be legally accurate, so help me Clinton."

•••

The Supremes' Greatest Hits

Thanks to a political science professor at Northwestern University, we may all soon be once again enjoying the Supremes' greatest hits. Only this time, we're not talking Diana Ross, folks. We're talking Earl Warren! It's move over, Mary Wilson and Florence Ballard! Make way for Sandra Day O'Connor and Ruth Bader Ginsberg!

According to a recent article in USA Today, Northwestern University Political Science Professor Jerry Goldman has produced a CD-ROM featuring recordings of some 70 hours of oral arguments before the U.S. Supreme Court. The CD-ROM is entitled The Supreme Court's Greatest Hits and is now available in computer stores across America.

Thanks to Professor Goldman, Supreme Court fans everywhere can now sit at their personal computers and click on and listen to the oral arguments in such historic Supreme Court cases as U.S. v. Nixon, Roe v. Wade and even Jerry Falwell v. Hustler Magazine.

Professor Goldman hopes that The Supreme Court's Greatest Hits will be a big hit among America's law students and perhaps undergraduate political science students as well.

But I think Professor Goldman is being far too short-sighted in his marketing plans for The Supreme Court's Greatest Hits. Goldman is sitting on a goldmine. With the right kind of marketing, his Supreme Court's Greatest Hits could be a hit not only in America's law schools, but in millions of homes across America as well.

All it takes is some creative marketing. Specifically, I think Professor Goldman should buy commercials on late night cable TV. The commercials could go something like this:

> K-Tell presents The Supreme Court's Greatest Hits! Now relive the wonderful memories of all the great Supreme Court decisions of your lifetime! Remember these great

judicial hits?

Brown v. Board of Education featuring Thurgood 'Soul Man' Marshall!

Gideon v. Wainwright, featuring the incomparable Abe Fortas!

U.S. v. Nixon, featuring James St. Clair and Elliott 'The Saturday Night Massacre Man' Richardson!

You'll also hear *Roe v. Wade*, the 1973 abortion decision, with its compelling background music, Paul Anka singing "She's Having my Baby."

If you order now, you'll also hear Justice Clarence Thomas and Professor Anita Hill singing their classic 1991 hit, "Reunited."

Or how about this judicial oldie-but-goodie? Tony Scalia and Dawn singing their all-time favorite, "Tie a Yellow Ribbon Round the Old Fourth Amendment!"

You'll hear the incomparable Justice Potter Stewart reciting his unforgettable line, "I can't define pornography, but I know it when I see it!"

And speaking of pornography, if you order now, you'll hear Ken Starr giving a compelling reading of his judicial romantic classic, *The Starr Report*, accompanied by the legendary Jose Feliciano, singing "Light My Fire!"

For a limited time only, if you order now, you'll also get the U.S. *Supreme Court Report* swimsuit edition, with a revealing look at Attorney General Janet Reno frolicking in the Reflecting Pool in front of the Washington Monument!

You'll also get the official Supreme Court Shoe Phone, a beautiful black Oxford wingtip from the Air Nixon Designer Shoe Collection!

Don't miss this once-in-a-judicial-lifetime opportunity! Forget about saying, "May it please the court!" For once, let the court please you with this 70-hour stroll down jurisprudential memory lane!

Call now! Our operators and our law clerks are standing by!

•••

Post-Traumatic Memories of Law School

A quarter century ago, Gerald Ford was president of the United States, Muhammad Ali was heavyweight champion of the world, and I was a first year law student at the University of Tennessee. I was probably the greenest, most unprepared student ever admitted to law school.

Several years ago, a newspaper reporter was writing a story about the life of the legendary baseball player, Yogi Berra. The reporter interviewed Yogi's first grade teacher and asked her whether Yogi was a good student. She replied, "Well, no. Not only did Yogi not know anything, he didn't even *suspect* anything."

Well, I was the Yogi Berra of my law school class. Not only did I not know anything, I didn't even suspect anything.

To this day, I am still not quite sure how I was admitted to law school. It must have been under Proposition 48. In any event, I'm sure I should have been red-shirted during my first year of law school.

I still vividly remember my very first day of law school and the first class I ever attended. The class was called "Contracts I" and was taught by a delightful fellow named Joseph G. Cook.

Based on my undergraduate experience, I expected Professor Cook to walk into the classroom, greet us all with a warm smile, and then spend the first class session introducing himself and telling us about the course we would study for the next several weeks.

But instead, Professor Cook walked into the classroom, dropped a huge textbook on the podium, and then glared at the class with all the warmth and happiness of a man who was suffering from a case of terminal hemorrhoids. And then I heard the following words come out of Professor Cook's mouth: "A offers to sell Blackacre to B for … "

I suddenly went into a panic because I hadn't the slightest idea what the word "Blackacre" meant. I assumed it was some brand of chainsaw.

To my horror, Professor Cook began to call on some of my fellow inmates, or rather classmates, and ask them questions, all involving A trying to sell something called "Blackacre" to B.

In desperation, I turned to my buddy, Cliff Knowles, who was sitting beside me. "What in the heck is a Blackacre?" I frantically whispered to Cliff.

Cliff, a Vandy grad who would go on to be editor-in-chief of the *Law Review*, calmly replied, "You know, Blackacre. It's like the name of a farm."

Well, of course. Blackacre. Sort of like Green Acres, the farm that that great lawyer Oliver Wendell Douglas bought on that TV show I used to watch when I was a kid.

Throughout the rest of the class, I sat in sheer terror, waiting for friendly Professor Cook to call on me. To make matters worse, during this whole time, the dad-blasted *Green Acres* theme song kept blaring through my mind.

I kept hearing Eddie Albert and Eva Gabor singing, "The chores! The stores! Fresh air! Times Square!"

After Contracts class ended, I stumbled across the hall to my first Property class, where so help me, a professor by the name of Dr. Overton performed a tap dance routine.

Worse yet, I suddenly noticed that among my classmates were several Eddie Haskell-types who kept waving their hands, volunteering to answer the tap-dancing professor's questions. These dweebs couldn't wait to use terms like "fee tail" and "executrix" and "seisin" (as in "It's football seisin!").

Heck, these guys not only knew what "Blackacre" meant, but their daddies probably owned Blackacre.

I was totally unprepared for this, because even as a first year law student, I had very little idea what lawyers actually did for a living. There were no lawyers in my family. I come from a long line of preachers. In fact, folks in my family firmly believe that the Lord calls preachers, and the Devil calls lawyers.

Consequently, my knowledge of law prior to enrolling in law school in the fall of 1975 was limited to what I had picked up by watching *The Perry Mason Show*, once a week from 1957 to 1966. However, I could not remember one episode where either Perry, Hamilton Burger, Della Street or Paul Drake ever used the work "Blackacre."

Well, thanks to the good Lord above, I managed to survive not only that first day of law school but to stumble through the next three years and somehow obtain a law degree. As the old joke goes, some folks graduate *Summa Cum Laude*, some folks graduate *Magna Cum Laude*, and some of us graduate Thank You, Laude. In my case, it was Laude Have Mercy.

Twenty-five years later, I still suffer from law school post-traumatic stress disorder. I have this recurring dream in which the dean calls me on the telephone and says, "Bill, I'm afraid we have some bad news. It appears there was an error on your transcript from the fall quarter of 1975, and you need to come back and re-take Professor Cook's Contracts class."

I pray this nightmare will never become a reality. But if it does, I intend to be ready. If Professor Cook asks me about Blackacre, I'm gonna tell him that it's probably the best brand chainsaw money can buy.

•••

Warning: The Attorney General has Determined That Automatic Lawyer Machines are Dangerous to our Profession

My fellow lawyers, I feel it is my duty to warn you about the greatest threat facing the legal profession today. I'm referring, of course, to "ALMs," the automatic lawyer machines.

According to an article in the ABA *Journal*, new-fangled devices called "QuickCourt" machines have recently been installed at courthouses in Arizona. These machines are similar to the ATMs (automatic teller machines) that can be found at most banks across America. According to the ABA *Journal*, QuickCourt is an "interactive computer system housed in kiosks similar to cash station machines." Courthouse shoppers can use QuickCourt to "produce completed legal forms for no-fault divorces, landlord-tenant cases, and small claims cases."

The proliferation of QuickCourt and other ALMs may sound harmless. But don't be naive. In the brave new world of ALMs, you and I could soon be replaced by Robo-lawyer.

That's right, folks. With automatic lawyer machines like QuickCourt, our clients will never have to come to our offices again. They can just drive by the courthouse, hop out of the car, and get easy legal services by punching a few buttons on the old interactive computer video screen.

For example, suppose Joe and Suzy Sixpack want a divorce. No need to waste time on real lawyers and judges. No, Suzy and Joe can just step up to the ALM and touch the divorce button. The ALM screen will then display the "Divorce Litigation Menu," and Joe and Suzy can select such grounds as "Irreconcilable Differences," "I caught her messing around," or "He snores all night and belches out loud all day!"

Joe and Suzy will punch a few more buttons, and faster than you can say "Elizabeth Taylor," the ALM will process a divorce. Within minutes,

Suzy, unlike Tammy Wynette, will no longer be standing by her man, not to mention her lawyer.

As if the ALMs aren't bad enough, consider this: A clerk's office at a courthouse in Miami has recently installed a drive-by window for filing and processing claims and other pleadings.

If this trend continues, before you know it, every courthouse in America will not only have ALMs, but they will also have judges sitting in drive-by windows, dispensing justice in much the same manner that McDonald's and Wendy's sells cheeseburgers.

Driver (speaking into microphone): "Let me have a no-fault divorce and a fill-in-the-blanks-will to go!"

Judge in Window: "Do you want fries with that?"

I can imagine the signs outside the courthouse: "McJustice. Over one billion litigants served!"

Well, my fellow lawyers, to borrow a phrase from that imminent jurist Barney Fife, it's time to nip this thing in the bud! We've got to stop QuickCourt, fast food justice drive-by courtrooms, and all those other automatic lawyer machines before we real lawyers go the way of the dinosaur.

Let's not make the mistake all those now-unemployed bank tellers made and be replaced by a bunch of interactive computer kiosks!

I say it's time that all the lawyers, judges and court clerks of America come together in righteous indignation! We should all write President Clinton (after all, he's a lawyer) and demand that he ban ALMs, drive-by courtrooms, and all other diabolical devices of fast food justice!

Better yet, let's write somebody really powerful, like Hillary or Janet Reno, or maybe even Regis and Kathie Lee.

•••

SECTION VI

It's Litigation Time in Tennessee!

The NCAA is No Match for Jerry Falwell and His Lawyers

Hallelujah, football fans! Thanks to Reverend Jerry Falwell and his lawyers, college football players can once again hold prayer meetings in the end zone! In the face of an all-out blitz from Liberty University's minister of defense and a host of lawyers, those agnostics at the National Collegiate Athletic Association have rescinded their Thou-Shalt-Not-Pray-After-A-Touchdown Rule.

Several years ago, the NCAA Rules Committee tackled the difficult issue of how scholarship student athletes should behave on the football field after scoring a touchdown. The problem is that over the last several seasons, most college football players have started to behave like professional wrestlers. After scoring a touchdown or making some other "big play," your typical college football player struts around as if he were a male peacock at the height of mating season. He shakes his fists at his opponents and walks around the field thumping his chest like Tarzan. And then for good measure, he celebrates his touchdown run by doing a little dance in the end zone as if what he really wanted to be in life was not a college football player, but a Michael Jackson impersonator.

Among the worst offenders have been those outstanding scholarship student athletes at the University of Miami. After scoring a touchdown, the entire Hurricane football team parades into the end zone and lines up and dances as if they were the Rockettes at Radio City Music Hall.

Worse yet, in recent years college football players have developed this ridiculous habit of taking off their helmets after big plays so that we football fans can see their faces. For some reason every college football player in America is of the opinion that we football fans are just dying to see their faces. Wide receiver Bubba Joe Baxter gallops into the end zone to put the State University Fighting Anteaters ahead in the

Weedeater Bowl, and suddenly young Bubba yanks off his helmet so that millions of us can see his pimply scholarship student athlete's face. I don't know how you feel, but whenever I see a college football player score a touchdown, I immediately jump up from my sofa, and scream out, "All right! Now, let me see that boy's face!"

Well, in a desperate attempt to restore some degree of humility to college athletics, the NCAA recently passed a rule forbidding players from engaging in certain types of unsportsmanlike conduct in the celebration of big plays. Among the forbidden activities were removing your helmet, taunting your opponents, dancing the Watusi, and otherwise engaging in activity that "calls attention to the player."

It sounded like an altogether sensible rule. However, it overlooked the highly-explosive issue of post-touchdown prayer meetings. The problem is that while some college football players choose to celebrate touchdowns by dancing in the end zone as if they were one of the Four Tops, other college football players prefer to pause after a touchdown and hold a brief Billy Graham Crusade in the end zone. This is particularly true at Reverend Jerry Falwell's Liberty University, where his football team, the Fighting Baptists, stop after each touchdown to pray briefly in the end zone while the Liberty University band plays a march version of "Just As I Am."

But the NCAA's new sportsmanship rule was interpreted to ban post-touchdown prayers in the end zone. Faster than you could sing "Drop Kick Me Jesus Through the Goalpost of Life," end zone prayers were forbidden, even at Notre Dame.

This did not sit well with either the Lord *or* Jerry Falwell. The Lord apparently spoke to Brother Falwell in a very clear voice and said, "Jerry, call your lawyers." Brother Falwell did so, and after he and his lawyers prayed about the matter, Brother Jerry announced that the Liberty University lawyers were ready to sue the football pants off the National Collegiate Athletic Association.

Well, the NCAA is no match for the Lord, Jerry Falwell, and a bunch of lawyers. Those agnostics on the NCAA Rules Committee issued a "clarifying memo" stating that it was okay for football players to kneel down and say a brief prayer to the Big Quarterback in the Sky after scoring a touchdown.

So there you have it, football fans. This season there will be no more dancing or impromptu rap concerts performed in the end zone after touchdowns. There will be no more strutting and taunting by college football players as if they were about to take on Hulk Hogan in a World Wrestling Federation heavyweight fight. There will be no more removing of helmets so that we can all see just how handsome this year's Heisman Trophy winner is. But thanks to Brother Jerry Falwell and his lawyers, college football players can still thank the Lord for a touchdown.

•••

The Manning Mooning

Not long ago, a student at the University of Tennessee engaged in a time-honored college tradition called "mooning." Following a distinguished academic exercise practiced by generations of scholars, the student bent over, briefly lowered his trousers, and exposed his scholarly fanny.

Like most moonings, the incident was supposed to be just a little college fun. Unfortunately, however, it turned out to be the most expensive moonshot since Apollo 13. The fanny in question in this mooning incident belonged to a student named Peyton Manning. As every college football fan knows, young Mr. Manning's main extra-curricular activity was not mooning people, but rather playing college football. He was so good at this activity (football, not mooning) that he may have been the best college football quarterback since Warren Moon.

The moonshot incident arose when young Mr. Manning was joking around in the football training room with a fellow male athlete in one of those towel-snapping, male-bonding sessions often engaged in by student-athletes. At a particular point in the jocularity, young Mr. Manning decided to, as the collegians are fond of saying, "drop trou," exposing his rear to his fellow male athlete. Unfortunately, unbeknownst to young Mr. Manning, there was a 27-year-old female trainer also present in the training room. The woman caught a glimpse of Manning's fanny when she was an unintended, inadvertent recipient of the Manning Moon.

Now you would think that a 27-year-old woman who works full time as a trainer in a university athletic department would not exactly be surprised to see a guy's rear end parading around a training room. But unfortunately, the sight of the Manning Moon was apparently a pretty traumatic experience for the young woman. She was so distraught that she took a leave of absence from the University's staff and filed a charge of gender discrimination against the University.

There must have been more to this incident than met the trainer's eyes because the University recently announced it was paying the young woman $300,000 in settlement of her complaint.

Well, I guess I shouldn't be shocked that the going price for seeing an All-American quarterback's fanny is $300,000, or $150,000 per cheek. After all, a jury ordered McDonald's to pay a woman $3 million because a cup of hot coffee spilled on her. And more recently, a lady in California sued Disneyland after her children suffered the traumatic experience of watching a Disneyland employee dressed as Mickey Mouse take off his mouse head. It could have been worse. Mickey could have mooned the kids.

In any event, young Mr. Manning apologized for the mooning and promised to keep his football pants up in the future. The female trainer has $300,000, which will no doubt help her cope with her post-traumatic stress disorder in the future as she relives the nightmare of the Manning Moon.

I don't know whether the young woman intends to continue her career as an athletic trainer. But if she does, let's just hope and pray she never sees another man's rear end for the rest of her life.

•••

Little League Ballplayers Need Big League Lawyers

Forty years ago, I played shortstop for the Cardinals. No, not the St. Louis Cardinals, but the Dellwood Baptist Church Cardinals, a little league team that played on a sandlot field of dreams in north Memphis.

The Dellwood Baptist Cardinals wore red and white uniforms just like the St. Louis Cardinals. We played against other little league teams who called themselves the Giants, the Tigers, the Dodgers, or the Yankees, and wore uniforms similar to those of their big league counterparts.

I loved my Cardinal uniform. In the summer of 1960, I wore it every day, even when we Cardinals had an "off day." I would put on my uniform and stand in front of my mother's full-length mirror, imagining myself stepping up to the plate at Busch Stadium. My little league uniform looked exactly like the St. Louis Cardinals' uniform worn by my hero, Stan the Man Musial. Well, not exactly. On the back of my Cardinals uniform were the words, "Bulldog's Barber Shop." Bulldog was a neighborhood barber who sponsored our team. I guess you might say he was the Gussie Busch of the Dellwood Baptist Cardinals.

As far as I know, Stan the Man Musial did not have the name of a barber shop on the back of his jersey. Nevertheless, in my Cardinals uniform, I felt I was the tobacco spittin' image of Stan the Man.

When I would come up to bat for the Cardinals in a big inning against the Schoolfield Methodist Church Pirates, I would get in a stance just like Stan the Man. I couldn't hit like Stan the Man, but I sure dressed like him, and I would try to hold the bat like him.

I thought I looked just like Stan the Man. Of course, Stan the Man was over six feet tall, while Billy the Boy was barely five feet tall in his hightop U.S. Keds.

I looked more like Stan the Munchkin than Stan the Man.

In those days, most big league ballplayers chewed tobacco. I and my fellow Dellwood Baptist Cardinals tried to emulate that as well. Before we would take the field against an opponent such as Jim's Texaco Orioles, my teammates and I would stuff as many as 27 pieces of Bazooka® bubble gum into our mouths so that we would have a big wad of bubble gum chewing tobacco in our jaws when we came to bat. I would even spit a little Bazooka bubble gum tobacco juice on the ground as I came to the plate, just I had seen Nellie Fox do when he would come to bat for the White Sox. That's the Chicago White Sox, not the Raines Drug Store White Sox.

It was great dressing up like a big league ballplayer when I was eight years old. Now that I'm a middle-aged daddy who couldn't even qualify as a replacement player, I enjoy watching my six-year-old son play tee-ball. But I hope that this spring my six-year-old and his teammates don't plan to dress up like the St. Louis Cardinals. If they do, I and the other players' dads will have to fork over some money to major league baseball owners.

Believe it or not, major league baseball has gone after sporting good stores that sell little leaguers unlicensed uniforms containing major league nicknames. Major league officials claim that they own the trademark for all major league nicknames, and if little leaguers want to dress up like big leaguers and use big league team names, they will have to purchase uniforms officially licensed by major league baseball and pay as much as six dollars more a uniform for the privilege.

That's right, baseball fans. Those same greedy folks who cancelled the 1994 baseball season and a World's Series, now want to make sure that kids across America shell out extra bucks for the privilege of dressing up like a major league ballplayer. Say your little boy wants to dress up like Cal Ripkin of the Orioles? Well, just have him send his piggy bank to major league baseball owners so that they can shake out six bucks worth of pennies!

Say your little girl's tee-ball team wants to call themselves the

Braves? Well, be sure to pay for that privilege. You wouldn't want Ted Turner's lawyers suing your little girl for trademark infringement, now would you?

You and I don't have to worry about little kids across America pretending to be major league baseball players in unlicensed uniforms. Heaven forbid!

Forty years ago, as a little league baseball player, I learned about such major league qualities as teamwork, commitment, and discipline. And now, my sons and other little leaguers of the 21st century can learn all about another quality of major league baseball … Greed.

•••

We Menfolk are No Longer Laughing Matters!

Here is a word of warning for you female readers who are about to head for the office. Be mighty careful what kind of jokes you tell today as you're standing around the old water cooler or enjoying a coffee break with your co-workers. If you tell a joke that offends one of your male co-workers, you might just find yourself a defendant in legal proceedings before the Equal Employment Opportunity Commission.

If you don't believe me, just ask Ruth Pierce.

Ruth Pierce is a female-type person who has a very important job. She's the national director of the Equal Employment Opportunity Office of the Social Security Administration. She is an expert on the general topic of "sexism in the workplace" and the particular topic of what kind of jokes can get somebody in a heap of legal trouble.

Ms. Pierce was the featured speaker at a Social Security Administration "diversity conference" in Miami. According to published news reports, Ms. Pierce decided to start off her speech with a joke. The joke went something like this: A man who was fishing caught a magic mermaid. The mermaid told the fisherman she could grant him a wish. The fisherman wished he were five times smarter. In response to this wish, the mermaid instantly turned the man into a woman.

Get it? Women-type people are five times smarter than us menfolk. A real knee-slapper. Hardy-har-har!

One of the people who was in the audience at the diversity conference and therefore heard Ms. Pierce's joke was a Social Security Administration employee named John Boyer. Mr. Boyer, a life-long member of the male gender, was not amused. Worse yet, he was offended by what he believed to be a sexist remark.

Mr. Boyer was so incensed and no doubt wounded by Ms. Pierce's joke that he made a complaint to the Commissioner of the Social Security Administration, demanding that Ms. Pierce be demoted and that she be required to issue an apology to all 65,000 Social Security Administration employees, including not only the smart female-type employees, but also the dumb male-type employees who are, of course, the real victims of Ms. Pierce's incredibly insensitive and sexist sense of humor.

Well, to paraphrase a line from that famous male astronaut, Neil Armstrong, this is one small step for man and one giant setback for laughter.

Thanks to the political correctness movement, we Americans now tell jokes at our peril. The political correctness speech police are constantly on the lookout for insensitive Americans who tell jokes that might offend women, ethnic groups, minorities, or household pets. And now, we can add menfolk to the protected class of those sensitive Americans who should not be the subject of jokes.

Well, I'm a life-long member of the male gender and proud of it, and I have to say I'm not the least bit offended by Ruth Pierce or any lady-type person who tells a joke about us menfolk.

Don't get me wrong. I don't think Ms. Pierce's joke was very funny. But this doesn't mean that Ms. Pierce is sexist or insensitive, or that she promotes a "hostile work environment for men." It just means the old gal can't tell a joke. She's obviously no Henny Youngman. She's not even a Henny Young-person.

The point is women are not as funny as men. Yeah, that's it. We men may not be as smart as women, but we sure are a lot better at telling jokes. And if that comment offends any of you female readers, then you're as big a hypersensitive wimp as is Mr. John Boyer of the Social Security Administration. I say it's time for you, Mr. Boyer, and the PC speech police to lighten up.

By the way, did you hear the one about the male federal employee at NASA who got fired by his female boss? The problem is every time she'd say, "Launch!," he'd go out to get a bite to eat.

•••

Can We "Save" the Ten Commandments?

Suddenly, all across America, millions of people are talking about the Ten Commandments. No, not the old movie starring Charlton Heston. People are talking about the original, honest-to-God, etched-in-stone Ten Commandments that the Lord gave to Moses during a summit conference at Mount Sinai several thousand years ago.

The burning theological question across America these days is: How can we "save" the Commandments that have long formed the bedrock of Judeo-Christian thought?

Recently over 20,000 people held a "Save the Ten Commandments Rally" in Montgomery, Alabama. At issue was a decision by a federal judge that the public display of a copy of the Ten Commandments in a state courthouse violates the United States Constitution by promoting a religion. Alabama Governor Fob James assured participants at the rally that he would do everything in his power to save the Ten Commandments, including ordering the National Guard and Alabama State Troopers to protect the public copy of the Ten Commandments if anyone tries to remove it. Thus, in Alabama, the Ten Commandments have actually been elevated to the level of the late legendary football coach Bear Bryant who always had state troopers standing around protecting him, particularly during dangerous situations such as the Auburn game.

Meanwhile, in Tennessee, state lawmakers debated a proposed law that would require all businesses that are open to the public to display copies of the Ten Commandments to their patrons. One can just imagine sitting down at a restaurant table and being confronted by a waiter who says, "Hi, My name is Jason and I'll be your waiter today. Our special today is the Fettuccine Alfredo. Oh, and the Commandment today is, 'Thou Shalt Not Covet Thy Neighbor's Wife.'"

Meanwhile, more liberal groups are trying to "save" the Ten

Commandments by updating them to be, shall we say, more politically-correct. For example, a priest in the Church of England recently announced that the Eighth Commandment — Thou Shalt Not Steal — should be modified to read, "Thou Shalt Not Steal Unless You're Stealing from a Greedy Corporate Chain." Father Robin Hood said the Lord doesn't mind us shoplifting from huge corporate groceries or department stores since those stores have already stolen from us.

In other words, "Thou Shalt Not Steal ... Except from Wal-Mart."

Presumably, Father Robin Hood will soon produce a whole set of new-and-improved politically-correct Ten Commandments, including the following:

"Thou Shalt Not Commit Adultery, Unless You and Your Spouse are Separated and the Act of Adultery Would Really Help You Build a Stronger Relationship in the Long Run."

"Honor Your Father and Mother, Unless You are Offered a Large Sum of Money to Appear on *Geraldo* or *The Jenny Jones Show* to Tell the Whole World Just How Mean and Terrible Your Parents Were to You."

"Thou Shalt Not Commit Murder, Unless You Can Afford to Hire Johnnie Cochran."

Well, maybe I'm naive, but I believe the Ten Commandments will survive this assault by an unholy alliance of federal judges, theologians, and politicians, even without around-the-clock protection from the Alabama National Guard, state troopers, or the Highway Patrol.

After all, the Ten Commandments have survived an awful lot over the years. If you don't believe it, consider this: According to Exodus, Chapter 32 (the non-politically-correct version, that is), the first edition of the Ten Commandments was lost when Moses broke the original tablets following his descent from Mt. Sinai.

That's right, Brothers and Sisters. Moses broke the Ten Commandments, and folks have been breaking them ever since.

•••

SECTION VII

But Seriously, Folks ...

How a Couple of Mountain Lawyers Saved the Constitution

In the spring of 1973, I was an undergraduate majoring in Football Appreciation at the University of Tennessee. Like a lot of college students, I skipped several classes that spring, and I've got the transcript to prove it.

But I didn't cut class in May of 1973 to throw a frisbee or to enjoy springtime in the mountains of East Tennessee.

No, I skipped several classes that spring so that I could sit in front of my black-and-white TV in my apartment and watch a couple of mountain lawyers save the Constitution of the United States.

At first glance on my TV screen, these two mountain lawyers had little in common. One was old; the other young.

One was a life-long yeller-dog Democrat. The other was a born-and-baptized Republican, the son of a GOP congressman.

One was from North Carolina, and the other was from Tennessee.

One had gone to Harvard. The other had gone to the University of Tennessee, and therefore in my impartial opinion, was the better-educated.

But they had two things in common. First, they were both from small towns in the mountains of the southeast United States. And like most mountain people, they had a strong sense of history and a commitment to their faith, their families and their friends.

And second, they were both trial lawyers. They had both spent many years of their lives trying cases before juries comprised of mountain folks. And based on that experience, both men had enormous respect for the common sense and fairness of ordinary people, particularly when they are brought together to resolve a dispute.

Fate cast these two mountain lawyers to sit side by side in a nationally-televised trial in the spring of 1973. The trial didn't take place in a courtroom. It took place in a hearing room in the U.S.

Capitol in Washington.

But make no mistake about it, it was a trial all right.

The "defendant" was the incumbent president of the United States who had just been re-elected in the greatest landslide in American political history.

And the jury? Well, I served on that jury, along with about 50 million other Americans who watched the televised hearings.

As the trial went on through the spring and into the summer of 1973, the two mountain lawyers did what trial lawyers do best. They asked incisive questions and made incisive comments.

The best questions were asked by the young mountain lawyer from Tennessee. It was his "cross-examination" that posed the central question of the time: "What did the president know and when did he know it?"

And the best comments were made by the old mountain lawyer from North Carolina. For many weeks, the old mountain lawyer listened to the testimony of many young "city lawyers" who had obstructed justice and had violated the public trust in pursuit of their own ambition. Finally, after hearing enough, the old mountain lawyer made a little speech. It was probably similar to the speeches he had made in North Carolina courtrooms for many years. It went like this:

> The evidence thus far introduced or presented before this committee tends to show that men upon whom fortune has smiled benevolently and who possess great financial power, great political power, and great governmental power, undertook to nullify the laws of man and the laws of God for the purpose of gaining what history will call a very temporary political advantage.
>
> But I come from a state where they have great faith in the fact that the laws of God are embodied in the King James version of the Bible, and I think those who partic-

ipated in this effort to nullify the laws of man and the laws of God overlooked one of the laws of God which is set forth in the seventh verse of the sixth chapter of Galatians: "Be not deceived. God is not mocked; but whatsoever a man soweth, that shall he also reap."

By the end of the summer of '73, the answers to the young mountain lawyer's persistent questions had emerged. And approximately a year later, for the first time in history, an American president resigned from office.

The old mountain lawyer was named Sam Ervin. The young mountain lawyer was named Howard Baker.

They represented the legal profession at its very best.

And during that remarkable spring and summer of 1973, they did nothing less than save the Constitution of the United States.

•••

Remembering John Glenn, Mrs. Gillespie and the Lord's Prayer

Nearly 40 years ago, on February 20, 1962, I was a fourth grader at Frayser Elementary School. My teacher, Mrs. Gillespie, turned on a large black-and-white TV set at the front of the class, and I and my classmates sat mesmerized as we watched Lieutenant Colonel John Glenn blast into orbit.

As the Atlas rocket soared upward, hurtling John Glenn 162 miles above the earth, Mrs. Gillespie proudly announced, "Children, this is a historic moment! For the first time in history, a man is orbiting the earth!"

At this point Benjamin Witt, the smartest boy in the class, quickly raised his hand and promptly corrected our teacher. "Actually, Mrs. Gillespie," Benjamin said, "Russian cosmonaut Yuri Gagarin was the first man to orbit the earth. He did it last year." I'll never forget what Mrs. Gillespie said in response to Benjamin. Giving him a sharp glance, she slowly and emphatically said, "The Communists *say* he orbited the earth. But nobody saw it happen. And never forget, children, the Communists always lie!" That was the kind of wonderful teacher Mrs. Gillespie was. She could slap down Yuri Gagarin, the lying Communists, and Benjamin The Smartest Boy in Class in one fell swoop.

Before she had turned on the TV set that morning so that we could all watch John Glenn go into orbit, Mrs. Gillespie had led our class in reciting the Lord's Prayer. She did this every morning. A few months later, in June of 1962, the United States Supreme Court ruled that Mrs. Gillespie was violating the United States Constitution when she led us in the Lord's Prayer. Actually, Mrs. Gillespie wasn't a defendant in the case, and I don't believe that Chief Justice Earl Warren ever called her and told her to quit praying. But even if he did, it wouldn't have made any difference. Mrs. Gillespie wasn't afraid of either Communists or

Supreme Court Justices. In fact, if Earl Warren or Nikita Khrushchev or Fidel Castro had ever appeared in our classroom, she probably would have spanked them right on the spot since she not only believed in the Lord's Prayer, she also believed in corporal punishment. In her case, however, it was more like major general punishment rather than corporal punishment since Mrs. Gillespie could deliver some fairly sharp licks to an unruly fourth grader's backside.

For nearly five hours on that cold February day in 1962, I and my classmates watched Walter Cronkite as he described each successful orbit of Friendship 7 until Lieutenant Colonel Glenn splashed down safely in the Atlantic Ocean.

By the end of that February day, I had a new hero. Suddenly, John Glenn ranked right up with my other icons such as Mickey Mantle, Johnny Unitas, and Ben and Adam and Little Joe and Hoss Cartwright.

That night after my parents put me to bed, I pretended that my bunk bed was Friendship 7. "Boy, that was a real fireball!" I exclaimed as I fired the retrorockets on my bunk bed and hoped that the heat shield would keep me from disintegrating in flames.

Well, all those wonderful memories from 1962 came back to me when Lieutenant Colonel — now — Senator John Glenn decided to do an encore. Thirty-six years after his last space flight, he once again blasted into orbit. It was one small step for man and one giant comeback for one of my childhood heroes.

I hadn't watched a NASA launch in years. But I didn't miss this one. I even recited the Lord's Prayer as I watched the lift-off. And as I wished Godspeed to John Glenn for the second time, I fondly remembered a time when I had a wonderful teacher and oh so many heroes.

•••

The Lawyer of Summer

On a warm spring day in May of 1972, Allie Prescott took the mound at Busch Stadium in St. Louis. He was number 65 in the resplendent white and red uniform of his all-time favorite team, the beloved St. Louis Cardinals.

It was a moment Allie had dreamed about since he was six years old and was the starting pitcher for the Prescott Memorial Baptist Church Little League team.

Growing up in the Berclair neighborhood of Memphis, Allie had dreamed time and time again that this moment in his life would some day come.

He dreamed about it during his years as a pitcher at Kingsbury High School.

He dreamed about it during the four years he played baseball for Memphis State, becoming an All-Missouri Valley Conference pitcher.

And he even dreamed about it during his three years at Memphis State University Law School.

There had been moments along the way when he felt the dream was about to become true. There was that moment when he was a high school senior at Kingsbury and was offered a contract by the Baltimore Orioles. The Orioles didn't offer much money, only a chance to pursue his dream. But as a high school senior, Allie had thought that the best way to pursue his dream was to accept a baseball scholarship to Memphis State. To Allie, it was only a dream delayed, not a dream declined.

He had thought the dream was coming true during his senior year at Memphis State, when he received yet another professional baseball contract offer, this time from the San Diego Padres. But again, he hadn't been offered much money, only a chance to play the game he loved. He had been accepted to Memphis State University Law School, and that offer frankly looked more realistic and more lucrative than the offer from the Padres.

But now, at long last, it seemed that his dream was about to become true. Allie really was there on the mound at Busch Stadium, just as he had always dreamed he would be.

There was only one catch. The stands were empty. There was no million dollar infield standing behind Allie as he stood atop the pitcher's mound. Directly behind him, center field was absolutely empty. Curt Flood was nowhere in sight.

The only ball players on the field were Allie, Cardinal utility catcher Bart Zeller, and Cardinals coach Vic Davilio.

It was not a major league baseball game. It was a tryout.

Allie was completing his final year at Memphis State University Law School. He was just days away from graduation, and was planning on joining a Memphis law firm. And then, he got a call from St. Louis.

Allie had been dating Kathy Sisler. Kathy's daddy was Dick Sisler, the legendary major league baseball player and a coach for the St. Louis Cardinals.

So here was the situation when Allie took the mound. His girlfriend had called her daddy who agreed to give Allie a tryout and a chance to make a dream come true.

For thirty minutes, Allie pitched to Vic Davilio while Coach Sisler looked on. Allie showed Sisler all the stuff he had developed since his years on the Memphis sandlots. He showed Sisler the fast ball he used to strike out the side against the Alta Vista Cardinals. He showed him the curve ball he had used against Treadwell and Overton High Schools.

He threw the slider that had led the Tigers to a victory over Louisville in Missouri Valley Conference play a few years earlier.

After a half hour of heat, the tryout ended. Allie Prescott, third year law student, was about to get the verdict.

Judge Sisler ruled quickly. "Son," he said. "If you want a chance to play, we'll sign you. But I've got to be honest with you. You've got good stuff, but I don't think it's good enough stuff. You'll play some in the minors, but I don't think you'll ever be back here."

Allie left Busch Stadium that day and headed back to Memphis to be a lawyer.

Minor league ballplayers have long referred to a brief appearance in the major leagues as "a cup of coffee." Allie hadn't had a cup. He only had a sip.

Seven years later, Allie was practicing law on the 25th floor of the One Hundred North Main Building in downtown Memphis as an associate with the firm of Thomason, Crawford & Hendrix. He was engaged to be married, but not to Kathy Sisler. He had found the real love of his life, other than baseball, Barbara Unger. He was getting ready to walk down the aisle, and he was prepared to spend his career as a trial lawyer.

And then, baseball called again. This time the call came from his old friend Dean Jernigan, then executive vice president for Fogleman Properties. Dean's boss, Avron, was the owner of the Memphis Chicks, the AA farm club of the Kansas City Royals. Dean asked Allie if he would agree to become general manager of the Chicks.

For several days, Allie struggled to make a decision. He had spent the last decade of his life in law, first as a law student, and then as a young lawyer establishing his career.

But he had already said "no" to baseball two times in his life. And he didn't want to say no again.

Allie went to his then senior partner, Frank Crawford, now presiding judge of the Western Section of the Tennessee Court of Appeals. He asked Frank what he should do. Allie would never forget Frank's response. "Go pursue your Walter Mitty dream, son," Frank advised him. "If it doesn't work out, you are always welcome back here."

For three years, Allie was general manager of the Memphis Chicks. They were the glory years in the history of the Chicks franchise, as record crowds packed Tim McCarver Stadium.

In 1981, Allie was named by the *Sporting News* ("the Bible of base-ball") as the minor league executive of the year.

Allie again was dreaming of the big leagues, hoping for the opportunity to be the general manager of a major league team.

And then, Allie and his bride had a little boy, Allie Prescott IV.

With no major league offers in sight and a growing family to feed, Allie decided it was time to return to law practice.

For over a year, Allie tried to establish a law practice as a sports agent representing professional athletes.

But Allie was restless and frustrated. He realized it would take years to establish himself as a sports agent, and his heart really wasn't in it.

His heart was still on that pitcher's mound in St. Louis. His heart was still with those hot summer nights at the ballpark with peanuts and popcorn and the organ playing "Take Me Out to the Ballgame" during the seventh inning stretch.

In 1984, Allie left law practice, and for the next 12 years, he devoted himself to public service, serving first as the executive director of the Memphis Park Commission, and then as executive director of the Memphis Metropolitan Interfaith Association, an ecumenical city-wide ministry for the poor. They were rewarding years for Allie and his family, particularly the years at Metropolitan Interfaith.

And then, in the fall of 1996, Allie got another call from his old friend Dean Jernigan. It wasn't just Jernigan calling. It was baseball calling, once again.

Jernigan, now the chief executive officer of Storage U.S.A., a Fortune 500 corporation, had a dream. He wanted to bring Triple A baseball to Memphis. Jernigan called Allie, just as if he were Tony

LaRusso summoning a relief pitcher from the bullpen. Jernigan asked Allie, "If I can get Memphis a new Triple A team, would you come back as general manager?"

For the fourth time in his life, baseball was calling Allie Prescott. For the second time in his life, Allie said yes.

In the winter of 1997, Memphis was awarded a AAA franchise, the new Memphis Redbirds.

And shortly thereafter, the new owners of the team, Christy and Dean Jernigan announced that they were going to build a beautiful new ballpark in downtown Memphis.

For the past three years, Allie has been more than just general manager for the Redbirds. He has been a visionary for his hometown, pursuing his dream of a ballpark that is more than just an athletic facility. It is a centerpiece for the renaissance and development of downtown Memphis.

On April 1, 2000, Allie Prescott was back on the field with the St. Louis Cardinals. But this time, he wasn't at Busch Stadium. He was on the beautiful new diamond of Autozone Park in downtown Memphis for the park's dedication ceremonies before the Cardinals played the Redbirds in an exhibition game.

Allie wasn't on the mound that day. But he was still pursuing his dream, just as he did on that warm spring day in 1972.

Finally, a postscript … Allie Prescott IV now attends Tulane University. Not surprisingly, he is a starting pitcher for the Tulane Green Wave.

On warm summer nights the two Allies, father and son, often sit together at the ballpark. From time to time, Allie the Dad gives his boy a little fatherly advice. It is simple and to the point: "I tell him," says Allie, "that he should always pursue his dreams. I tell him life is short. Don't rush things … Be happy."

•••

Why Lawyers Have Always Been My Heroes

Ever since the 1994 players' strike, lawyer-bashing has threatened to replace baseball as our official national past time. Indeed, many lawyers these days feel like Rodney Dangerfield. We get no respect, no respect at all.

Late night comedians in search of a cheap laugh always take digs at lawyers.

Two-bit politicians desperately seeking votes thoughtfully blame America's problems on the legal profession.

And thanks to the political correctness movement, there is only one group left in America that can properly be the subject of jokes: lawyers.

Nobody ever tells jokes about CPAs. (Question: Do you know what an actuary is? Answer: He's someone who does not have the personality to be a certified public accountant.)

But when late night comedians like Jay Leno take a cheap shot at lawyers, I just grab the remote control. (Heck, if I were like Elvis, I'd just whip out a pistol and shoot out the picture.)

And when statesmen (sic) like Dan Quayle attack lawyers, I just remind myself that most lawyers know how to spell "potato."

I don't care what the comedians or the politicians say about the legal profession. Lawyers are now and have always been my heroes.

Lawyers first became my heroes when I was a boy. One of the things I inherited from my father was a love of reading, particularly reading biographies. Within a couple of years after advancing from Dick and Jane and Sally and Spot, I began to read biographies of Clarence Darrow, Henry Clay, Abraham Lincoln and Daniel Webster, just to name a few.

By the fourth grade, after reading several of these biographies, I noticed that all of these great men had something in common. They were all lawyers.

They were also all men of courage. They were often advocates for unpopular people and unpopular causes. They didn't live their lives based on opinion polls or popularity contests. They were fearless advocates who in President Kennedy's marvelous phrase, mobilized the English language and sent it into battle on behalf of their clients.

These historical figures were inspirational to me. And they made me dream about growing up to be a lawyer.

In 1963, when I was 11 years old, I was inspired by another courageous lawyer, albeit a fictional one. I sat in the Northgate Theater in downtown Frayser, Tennessee, and watched a "picture show" (as we called them in those days) called *To Kill a Mockingbird*.

I will never forget the scene when Atticus Finch walked out of the courtroom after "losing" the trial in his defense of Tom Robinson. But Atticus wasn't a loser in my tear-stained eyes. He was a hero, and I wanted to grow up to be a lawyer just like him.

Nearly 40 years later, I don't claim to be a Clarence Darrow or an Atticus Finch. Nevertheless, my childhood dream has come true. I am blessed to be a trial lawyer, and there is at least one thing I do have in common with Darrow and Finch. Like both of them, I've lost some really big cases in my career.

And after 22 years of law practice, lawyers remain my heroes. Indeed, over the years, I have found more heroes to go along with Clarence and Atticus.

As a young lawyer, I had heroes such as Judge Billy Frank Crawford and Buddy Thomason who served as mentors for me about what a trial lawyer ought to be.

I've also had a hero named Al Harvey. That's Major General Al Harvey of the United States Marines, and he has always personified for me the patriotism and public service of our profession at its very best.

In May of 1981, I married a beautiful lawyer named Claudia Swafford, and through her, I found two more heroes. The first was my father-in-law, Howard Swafford, who is a veteran of World War II and the Korean Conflict and has been a country lawyer for over 50 years. And to paraphrase a line from Will Rogers, I've never met a country lawyer I didn't like.

The second hero Claudia introduced me to was my mother-in-law, Claude Swafford. Claude was one of only two women in her University of Tennessee Law School Class of 1948. When Claude was a first-year law student, she was confronted by the law school dean who told her in no uncertain terms, "You're not welcome here. You're only here to find a husband." (Funny, but when I was in law school and dating Claudia, the dean never approached me and said, "You're not welcome here. You're only here to find a wife.")

When Claude graduated, she continued to face adversity. Like Justice Sandra Day O'Connor, her first job was as a legal secretary because the gentlemen's club that was the Bar at that time would not hire her as a lawyer.

Well, in my impartial opinion, my mother-in-law is the best lawyer in the family. She's bold and outspoken and she never shies away from a fight.

Over the past two decades, I have grown to know many other "everyday heroes" of the legal profession. And if called as a witness, here is my testimony on their behalf: Over the past 22 years, I've seen countless lawyers devote thousands of hours to such unselfish endeavors as creating not-for-profit foundations, chairing community boards, and leading community efforts to help the poor, the sick, and the homeless.

I've seen lawyers at great personal sacrifice represent indigent inmates on death row in capital cases only to be viciously attacked in the court of public opinion.

I've seen lawyers lead churches, synagogues, civic groups, Boys Clubs and Girls Clubs.

I've seen lawyers coach little league baseball teams, lead scout troops, and build houses for Habitat for Humanity.

And I've heard lawyers speaking at inner-city public schools, attempting to inspire young women and young men to dream they might grow up to be lawyers just like one little boy I know dreamed nearly 40 years ago.

Winston Churchill once defined a professional as someone who not only makes a living, but also makes a life.

Measured by that marvelous standard, lawyers are the ultimate professionals. They make a living, but they also build a life for their families, their friends and their communities.

I've been blessed to share both a professional and personal life with such everyday heroes. My closest friends are lawyers, and the love of my life is a lawyer.

And I wouldn't mind at all if someday my three kids grew up to be lawyers … just like their momma.

•••

About the Author

Bill Haltom is a trial lawyer (not a litigator) with the firm of Thomason, Hendrix, Harvey, Johnson & Mitchell in Memphis.

He is chair of the Board of Editors of the ABA *Journal* and has served as president of the Memphis Bar Association and president of the Tennessee Bar Association Young Lawyers Division.

Bill's humor columns appear monthly in the *Tennessee Bar Journal* and weekly on the Tennessee Bar website, TBALink®, at www.tba.org.

Bill is the author of *Daddies: An Endangered Species*, a collection of his humor columns on the need for old-fashioned fatherhood.

He is married to Claudia Swafford Haltom, a Juvenile Court Referee judge in Memphis. Bill and Claudia have three children. Their real names are Will, Ken, and Margaret Grace. However, in Bill's columns he identifies them as Wally, Beaver, and Her Royal Highness the Princess.

About the Illustrator

David Jendras is the director of publication and new media for the ABA *Journal*, and he has served as president of the Society of National Association Publications.

David and his wife, Gerry, have three kids (a CPA, a veterinarian and a college student), one Collie and one Sheltie.

MR209TU